Millennial Keynes

Millennial Keynes

An Introduction to the
Origin, Development,
and Later Currents
of Keynesian Thought

Bruno Ventelou

Translated and edited, with an
introduction by Gregory P. Nowell

M.E.Sharpe
Armonk, New York
London, England

Library of Congress Cataloging-in-Publication Data

Ventelou, Bruno.
    [Lire Keynes et le comprendre. English]
    Millennial Keynes : an introduction to the origin, development, and later currents of
Keynesian thought / Bruno Ventelou; translated and edited, with an introduction by
Gregory P. Nowell.
      p. cm.
Translation of: Lire Keynes et le comprendre.
Includes bibliographical references and index.
ISBN 0-7656-0670-4 (alk. paper)
    1. Keynesian economics—Textbooks. I. Nowell, Gregory P. (Gregory Patrick), 1954–
II. Title.

HB99.7. V42613 2004
330.15'6—dc22   2003070437

Printed in the United States of America

The paper used in this publication meets the minimum requirements of
American National Standard for Information Sciences
Permanence of Paper for Printed Library Materials,
ANSI Z 39.48-1984.

BM (c)   10   9   8   7   6   5   4   3   2   1

Contents

Acknowledgments

Bruno Ventelou would like to thank his colleagues and mentors who helped with the French edition of this book, as well as the students who used early drafts of the manuscript in their coursework. Gregory Nowell would like to thank Alan Isaac, Gary Mongiovi, Fiona Machlachlan, Mine Doyran, and others who helped with the review of the manuscript, the preparation of this translation, and revisions of the introduction. Professors Ventelou and Nowell collaboratively rewrote some portions of this book, which in effect has become a second revised edition, rather than a direct translation.

Millennial Keynes

Introduction

Keynesian Economics and the American Polity

Gregory P. Nowell

> *Thus our argument leads toward the conclusion that in
> contemporary conditions the growth of wealth, so far from
> being dependent on the abstinence of the rich, as is
> commonly supposed, is more likely to be impeded by it. One
> of the chief social justifications of great inequality of
> wealth is, therefore, removed.*
> —Keynes, General Theory

The motivating spirit of Keynesian economics depends on two core ideas: that social equity is the key to making capitalism sustainable, and that to achieve social equity there must be a national commitment to full employment and to income redistribution. The emphases on employment and redistribution are direct reflections of the crises of the pre–World War II era, but we do no violence to Keynes in adding, in our own time, environmental protection and quality of life to the goal of social equity.

Keynes faced two sorts of international crises in his lifetime. The first was the collapse of the European economy after World War I.[1] Keynes argued passionately that excessive debt burdens in the wake of this war—not just the reparations imposed on Germany but debts contracted by all the nations of Europe—would crush their collective economies. His call for a "general bonfire" (*Economic Consequences of the Peace*, 281) of debt was an appeal to free Europe's laborers and capitalists from the catastrophic misjudgments of their governments. He darkly warned of tyrannies and communist experiments that would otherwise emerge, and in the event he was largely proved right.

At the same time, Keynes's other chief recommendation, that trade

3

liberalization in Europe would encourage economic recovery, anticipated contemporary policies. The United States and the International
Monetary Fund invariably respond to economic crises by pushing for
more trade liberalization. The thrust of Keynes's early arguments was
that, absent vindictive reparations policies and punitive trade restrictions on Germany, the natural force of capitalism would lead Europe
toward recovery from the crisis of the war.

Keynes's arguments in *Economic Consequences of the Peace* had rec-
ognizable liberal, in the sense of laissez-faire, ancestry. The victorious
Allied governments interested in postwar Europe's recovery needed only
to shed the irrational pursuit of measures designed to strangle Germany's
industrial potential. The underlying thought was similar to that of Smith
in the *Wealth of Nations*[2] or Kant in *Perpetual Peace*[3]: wealth and prosperity are the best guarantors of peaceful relations among states, and
governments ought not to pursue power at the expense of the collective
wealth that would best ensure security.

The second international crisis was the Great Depression. Here Keynes
dropped the premises that underlay the *Economic Consequences of the
Peace*. He came instead to the conclusion, common to more radical analyses of that time, that the economic system was not "self-remedying" and
did not have the natural impulse to recovery he had formerly imputed to
capitalism. The insights that Keynes developed in this period are really
the core of Professor Ventelou's valuable introductory book on Keynesian
economics and how it developed. Whereas World War I could leave
Keynes with the impression that an "exogenous shock"—war and its
aftermath—could be held accountable for the economic collapse, the
diagnosis in the pathbreaking *General Theory of Employment, Interest,
and Money* was that "endogenous shocks"—specifically a failure of investors to behave in a manner that optimized the output of goods and
services and thus employment—were an equally grave threat to capitalist economies.[4]

In both the early and later works, the tone of Keynes's arguments
contrasts sharply with the comparative complacency of most modern
economics: with the rise of the Soviet Union and the totalitarian fascist
economies, Keynes understood that capitalism itself was precariously
founded on its ability to deliver essential goods and services and to maintain itself in the face of grim social alternatives. His economic theory
presents itself not so much as the exposition of "eternal mathematical
laws" as the intellectual foundation for institutionalizing equity and full

employment as social goals. No intellectual in the 1930s, much less Keynes, could take "capitalism" for granted as a social system. It was therefore wise to explore the ways in which capitalism's production of goods and services could be optimized and made attractive enough to make it socially stable in the face of grave historical challenges.

Keynes died at the beginning of the era of American dominance, free trade, and comparative economic stability and peace. His life was dominated by the menacing growth of totalitarian empires that showed what can happen when the capitalist world falls apart, a point he did not fail to miss in *Economic Consequences of the Peace*, where he likened pre–World War I liberalism to El Dorado, Utopia, and, to round out the list, Paradise (6–7). This was a world overthrown by an evil serpent wielding "the projects and politics of militarism and imperialism, of racial and cultural rivalries, of monopolies, restrictions, and exclusion" (7).

In our time, with fifty years of capitalist growth behind us, the centrally planned economy of the old Soviet Union in ruins, and China a growing and puissant nation only to the extent that it has embraced capitalism, it is easier to succumb to the illusion that the capitalist system is "natural" and thus a historical inevitability.[5] Judging from the assault on workers' rights and security that has characterized Thatcherism in England and the new era of Republican dominance in the United States, it is now easy to envision a world in which social equity is not considered a valid goal of social policy, primarily because there are no looming threats to the capitalist order.

A world at peace appears to be a world in which triumphant capitalism makes it very difficult to advance a progressive agenda. It is unsettling to remember that before World War I, Keynes's El Dorado of international capitalism was a bustling commercial world of self-satisfied capitalists: there were only minimal concerns for social equity, and the threats from fascist or communist radicals were scarcely credible in the wealthy countries. It was a world very much like our own, where limited imperial adventures did not trouble the public imagination: Britain's seizure of South Africa was swallowed as easily as the United States' recent seizure of Iraq. Then and now there was an unshakable faith in the pursuit of business as the means to social progress. And it was precisely this complacent, fairly prosperous world that was rent by two generations of savage warfare and plummeted into the economic crisis of the Great Depression.

Keynesian economics should not be mistaken as a recipe for universal peace. But it sees prosperity and wealth as features of capitalism that must be carefully cultivated, an underlying attitude that makes it suitable not just for the trials of yesteryear but for those that lie before us. Capitalist societies with firm commitments to social equity seem, as a rule, to be more suited to the requirements of international citizenship—itself a concept, after all, rooted in traditional liberal theory.[6]

In the present period, the rhetorically dominant values of laissez-faire individualism and tax-cut antistatism are a consistent, though nightmarish, belief system.[7] In the new ideology, which is really a warmed-over old one, Social Security is seen negatively as a tax that discourages investment that creates jobs. Environmental regulation is also a tax and also discourages job creation, so it is better to "go slow" on improving the environment: let the utilities make acid rain. The anti-Keynesian state rests on a rather bleak view that exalts private accumulation and minimizes, under the antitax banner, the need for corporate accountability for public misbehavior.

The right to security in old age, the right to access to medical care, and the right to benign environmental technologies all have their advocates. Yet the defense of these policy goals takes place in a desultory fashion, and nowhere do we see it suggested that there is an underlying economic logic and philosophy that unites these themes, not merely as morally justified ways to cure capitalism's social inequalities, but as practical instruments to remedy the recurrent weakness of capitalism: the tendency of income to accumulate at the top of the social order, and the ensuing weakness in the entire economy that results.

It was a unified view of social entitlements that led to the welfare states of Europe and to the less committed welfare policies of the United States. The thirty to forty years in which these views prevailed created some of the most benign social conditions in human history. To understand why capitalism could flourish not in spite of, but because of, the commitment to social welfare, we need to contrast Keynes's approach to aggregate demand with the traditional view that funneling income to the upper classes is the means to create the savings that fuel investment.

All income in capitalist societies results from what consumers buy, or what businesses buy in order to produce, represented by Keynes (*General Theory* 1964, 63) thus: Income = Consumption + Investment.

Savings is money left over from income, after people buy what they want to buy: Income – Consumption = Savings.

Since Income – Consumption = Savings in our second term, and since rearranging the equation of the first term gives Investment as also equal to Income – Consumption, we arrive at: Savings = Investment.

This is one of the simpler arguments in the *General Theory*. It is true by definition (an accounting identity), but the exposition is already preparing us for a departure from traditional notions. For one might say—intuitively, but wrongly, in Keynes's view—that increasing savings will, by means of this accounting identity, increase investment and thus increase income. This is the neoclassical argument, and in various forms it dominates most public rhetoric ("we must increase private savings to fund the retirement of aging populations"). Indeed, even among progressive thinkers it was quite popular, in the 1980s, to argue that average Americans should increase their savings rate to equal that of people in Japan, if the United States were to recover economically from its stagnation.[8] Given the collapse of Japanese financial assets, and that country's anemic demand, low growth, and high savings rate, this view now seems quaint: it should serve as a reminder that we should not fall into an indolent neoclassicism when times are good and then snatch Keynes back from the shelf when times are bad.

For readers of Keynes, saving as the fuel of investment is a well-established analytic trap. As Keynes himself notes in the *General Theory*, the notion of saving as a private virtue that leads to the public good is very well established. Indeed, the early Keynes even cited virtuous saving as foundational to the European economy in the pre–World War I era: "If the rich had spent their new wealth on their own enjoyments, the world would long ago have found such a regime intolerable. But like bees they saved and accumulated, not less to the advantage of the whole community because they themselves held narrower ends in prospect."[9]

So it is that Keynes himself first appears as an anti-Keynesian. In spite of his own later repudiation of such notions, "tax cuts for the rich," whether in the 1980s or the first decade of the twenty-first century, have been justified with the trickle-down argument that since the rich spend less they save more, and that saving is good and will lead to investment. Thus the common people should make common cause with the rich to make sure that the rich get richer, which will lead to more jobs for more common people.

Indeed, tax cuts to benefit the rich have, in the United States, become a kind of public religion. In the brief era of the American budgetary surplus, tax cuts were needed because the government was accumulating money that was not "its own." In an economic downturn, the economy must be salvaged by inducing capitalists to invest. And any conceivable penalty on the saving of the rich must also be removed. Hence, no matter what the issue, the right offers only one economic policy, the tax cut, and the imbalance between government income and expenditure, formerly denounced by the right as irresponsible, has been transformed into a bizarre doctrine of pillaging the treasury in the name of the public welfare.

But Keynes did not see increasing saving as the remedy to deficient investment, and it followed that he could not, and did not, endorse the concentration of the wealth in the hands of the few. In fact, this view is anathema to Keynes's entire intellectual project. He argued that saving is an understandable impulse, but nonetheless an endemic problem for capitalist societies. Keynes reasoned that consumers who save money are sending a signal to businesses, and their investors, that there is a limited demand for their products. Savers are people who prefer to keep printed numbers in their wallets, or electronic numbers in their bank accounts, to enjoying real consumption items. Saving is in fact a "failure to consume." Smart capitalists therefore do not produce to meet the demand implied by people's total incomes. Rather, businesses hold back their production to the level of after-saving income that they anticipate will actually be spent. They restrict investment as a result. Fewer investment goods are bought with the idea of making something to sell to consumers. Stagnation or decline in the purchase of investment goods means fewer jobs. As a result, current income falls.

Thus, Keynesian economists characteristically believe that aggregate income diminishes as the desired level of saving increases. Or as Keynes himself wrote: "Every such attempt to save more by reducing consumption will so affect incomes that the attempt necessarily defeats itself" (*General Theory* 1964, 84).

Keynes thought that individuals had rational reasons for saving, but that the systemic result was at variance with the individual behavior. The purpose of saving is to make a person richer or, at least, to make a person feel richer. The collective result of too many people saving too much is a contraction of investment in the aggregate.

The contraction of investment diminishes the incomes out of which people save. Thus pessimism on the part of investors, seen as a group, is always self-fulfilling. If they are gloomy, they invest less, incomes fall, and total saving declines to the level of lower investment. If they are optimistic, they invest more, incomes rise, and increased saving is made possible by increased aggregate incomes. Investors are gloomy when people are saving: their propensity to consume is too low. Investors are optimistic if consumers are spending: their propensity to consume is high.

Keynes saw government intervention as a means to remedy a decline in the "marginal propensity to consume." While it cannot be ruled out that the whole population's consumption propensity will vary over time, generating macroeconomic changes as a result, Keynes followed the tradition of underconsumption theorists. One of the main causes of secular declines in the propensity to consume was the concentration of wealth: a rich person with a million dollars spends less of the total income than a thousand poor people with a thousand dollars each. The distribution of income is thus linked to the consumption propensity of the economy as a whole, and the economy's performance reflects political decisions about taxation and the distribution of wealth.

Conservatives argue that the decreasing marginal propensity to consume of the rich is good (their saving funds investment), whereas a more liberal view, that goes back even before Keynes, is that the savings rate of the rich is actually a social problem.[10] If the rich could be made to spend all their income, employment would be higher and society richer. The failure of the rich to consume justifies a policy of progressive taxation on their incomes.

Implementing redistribution, however, is much harder than theorizing about it. Thus the short phrase that identifies Keynesian economics is not "social welfare policies," which in fact follows from his arguments, but "budget deficits." The government has the ability to borrow vast sums of money and can make up for deficient demand. Thus, Income = Consumption + Investment + Government Spending. Weak consumption leads to weak investment, which leads to declining incomes and rising unemployment. Government spending spurs both consumption and investment, causing incomes to rise. Government spending may take the form of direct government production through state ownership and production, of production under contract, or of redistribution of income to those who will most likely spend it. Absent programs for the redistribution of income, government deficits work only to bolster an economy that will suffer recurring anemia due to insufficient demand.

The failure to have an aggressive social welfare policy to bolster demand is, in very real terms, not a moral failing but a precondition for the periodic episodes of weak demand and weak investment that make involuntary unemployment a recurring feature of market economies.

Nonetheless, the radical, "redistributive" feature of Keynes's thinking was subverted into the simple phrase "government deficits."[11] Since businesses borrow in order to invest, the notion that the government could make up for deficient private investment by itself borrowing had different implications than the notion that those with high savings rates should be taxed. The rich could be left alone and the government could borrow from them in order to invest what private investors would not invest themselves. Such borrowing jump-starts the economy and does not tamper with the underlying structure of power; indeed, with this kind of deficit spending, the rich get an alternative investment vehicle, government bonds, to take the place of the corporate bonds that they find unattractive because the poor business climate creates an atmosphere of high bankruptcy risk.

But, cut loose from its link to redistribution, government spending simply targets well-organized constituencies who have their hands out, and delivers only incidental income enhancement to the poorest strata with the highest propensity to consume.[12]

Some mid-twentieth-century Marxists argued that such deformations of Keynesian thinking were to be expected and that the reformist optimism of Keynesian New Dealers was misplaced.[13] Instead of programs to boost the disposable income of the poor, thereby creating the aggregate demand that would spur investment, they argued that government policy would focus on tax cuts for corporations, boosting their after-tax income and hoping that they would invest rather than save the extra funds. But this policy concentrates income precisely in the hands of the group that, Keynes warns us, has extremely volatile attitudes toward risk and investment. If the economy is faltering because of inadequate investment, giving wealthy corporations even more money to invest makes little sense, since they are not investing with the funds (or using the credit access) they already have.

Another leftist criticism of Keynesian thinking was the ability of Keynes's deficit-friendly theory to justify massive military expenditures. National defense has always had an "objective need" quality: when enemies are out there, not spending on defense is suicide. Deeply impressed by the huge government budgets that funded two world wars, Marxists argued that Keynesian theory was really the clothing that disguised imperialism as economic prosperity; war was the "capitalist solution" to economic crisis. This reasoning tied the thinking of the *General Theory* to the earlier ideas of J.A. Hobson. In his 1902 treatise *Imperialism: A Study*,[14] Hobson argued that redistribution of income is needed to make a capitalist economy work better, but at the same time he excoriated deficit spending as militaristic and a threat to the safety of nations. Abstract Keynesian theory, Marxist reasoning went, allowed military spending to transmute into a substitute for liberal social welfare policy.[15]

Nonetheless, events have outrun the neat packaging of the "military Keynesian" thesis. The United States today is widely viewed as an imperial power, not in the nineteenth-century mold but imperial nonetheless. Yet it spends only 4 percent of its gross national product on the military. That is down from 54 percent of net national output during World War II (a high reached in 1944),[16] and it must now be observed that if the United States engages in military adventures as it has in Iraq and Afghanistan, the reason is not that elites have cleverly rigged the budget to foster militarism to spur a flagging economy. Rather, the cost of such adventures is the national financial equivalent of pocket money: they are undertaken precisely because they are cheap—or at least appear so at first.

Hobson's "taproot" thesis (*Imperialism*, 71–109) that government expenditure may be rigged by elites to benefit themselves certainly is still relevant: there is nothing to preclude the possibility that oil interests and weapons makers dominate elements of American foreign policy and the military appropriations process. This is Hobson's "parasitism." But here we can speak of only special interests, not of imperialism as an aggregate demand-pushing macroeconomic policy. The U.S. welfare state (including Social Security), which by European standards is not particularly impressive for the scale or quality of its services, nonetheless is two to three times the military budget in economic significance and expenditure levels.

At first blush, the current political pattern in the United States confounds the traditional simplifications of Keynesian policy. The Republican Party forays boldly, in the 1980s and now, into the zone of immense fiscal deficits. The Democratic Party has been thrust into the position of defending apparent fiscal orthodoxy: balanced budgets.

Underneath the apparent contradiction is a partial understanding of Keynes.[17] Government deficits are merely one potential tool for the government to boost sagging demand and investment in the capitalist economy. A temporary increase in government spending would compensate a temporary decrease in investment. But such transitory policy ignores the need for more permanent welfare efforts directed at the marginal propensity to consume and the tendency of capitalist economies to weaken when consumption is less than unity, that is, when less than 100 percent of aggregate income is actually spent. Redistributing income to the poor is not an exercise in Christian charity; it is essential to keeping the economy afloat.

This basic tenet of the Keynesian approach has been confounded in recent years by U.S. statistics showing household savings rates declining to zero. After all, Keynes argued that it is the "decreasing propensity to consume" of the wealthy that poses the problem of unemployment for the poor. If net savings is zero or close, as it has been, then everyone ought to be working.

These aggregate statistics, however, conceal a vast discrepancy between the upper and lower classes of American society. The upper quintile of the American population is doing quite well in terms of income (earning 50 percent of all money income). The distribution of assets is even more unequal. Nine and a half million U.S. families have total net worth of $2.4 trillion. The other 93 million families share $3.8 trillion, and of those the bottom 7 million families have median net financial assets of precisely zero.[18]

Consumer debt tells another sobering story. Based on net assets, the bottom quintile of the American population has a consumer debt level (which excludes home mortgage but includes car and credit cards) whose median is $11,500 and average is $17,375. In the upper quintile, the median is $900 and the average is $5,340. The poor are obviously making expenditure finance choices that the well-to-do refuse.

The mass markets for consumer credit for the poor no doubt have generated billions in a temporary surge in expenditure. But these people, who have no cushion against personal misfortune and who will be very hard hit by recent changes to bankruptcy law, as a group are increasingly taking on the attributes of sharecropping debt peons. The debtor working class seems more and more similar to the sharecroppers formerly typical of the American South and today of the third world. Their consumption of goods and services must actually fall as a result of their need to service debt. So, even though their access to credit has pushed their expenditure levels higher than their net income, the middle- and long-term effect is to push their consumption to less, since henceforth their expenditure levels are Income – Debt Service = Consumption. The affluent, meanwhile, relatively untroubled by debt, conform to the traditional model of Income – Savings = Consumption, and they are the major beneficiaries of that astounding social welfare program for the affluent, the mortgage interest deduction, which reduces the cost of purchasing the principal nonfinancial asset, a home. Savings is thus a class characteristic of affluence, even if some upper quintile families cannot control their spending. The affluent get to purchase the bonds issued by the deficit-ridden government as a result of their own tax revolt against redistribution. Today's inadequate redistribution expenditures become a vehicle for further upward redistribution of wealth to the affluent as a class. They may also invest their savings either directly or through mutual funds in the bonds and stocks issued by the financial companies whose mass credit operations inflict misery upon the poor.

The near-zero personal savings rate of the United States thus does not point to the irrelevance of Keynes's warnings about the marginal propensity to consume. Rather, what has happened is that the grossly inadequate wage levels of the poor, and the stagnant wage levels of the middle-income quintiles, have been ignored as the economy has been temporarily doped to a higher level of expenditure through mass consumer credit. The price of this credit, after the initial spending impetus, is a decreased propensity to consume out of income and the relegation of millions of people to the hounding and harassment of computerized collection services on the theory that "they deserve it" because they spent irresponsibly. And the badge of bad debt is increasingly used to discriminate among people in the rental housing market and the employment market. This is simply a modernization of the traditional notion that the poor deserve hunger and disease because otherwise they would not be motivated to work, and that to be poor is a crime that deserves the punishment of social exile and unceasing humiliation.[19]

In short, mass consumer credit has created a nightmare version of Keynes's point that a society with low aggregate savings has a better chance at high overall employment than one with high personal savings (*General Theory* 1964, 126–127). Keynes did not address the novel idea that zero net savings could coexist with weak aggregate demand because no sane economist in 1936 could have foreseen a society with massive consumer debt, aggressively extended by a nation's leading financial institutions, accumulated by common wage earners and the lower strata of the poor. That is to say, he assumed a classical wage society, not a nation of debt slaves. Debt contracted by the poor exacerbates the consumption deficiencies that Keynes originally identified. The first obligation of the less affluent 80 percent that divides 50 percent of all income is to lessen their debt when and if their situation improves. Debt payback does not spur consumption. Therefore, in a recovery, increased consumer spending must come from those with the highest savings rate: the affluent. And yet these are precisely the ones who do not spend in the required degree.

Worse, more than in Keynes's time, the spending of the affluent quintile is geared to the performance of its financial assets and thus becomes what economists call "procyclical," an economic behavior that makes good times better, and bad times worse. The poor get a temporary spending boost from credit that ultimately lowers their net expenditures as they get mired in debt service. The low savings rate of the United States is a symptom of the massive income inequalities in the most economically unequal society in the industrialized world, one in which debt peonage for the multitude is the preferred alternative to adequate wages, universal access to medical care, and redistributive programs, including socially necessary expenditure on everything from schools to "green" alternative-fuel transportation systems. We have a huge consumer debt and a large government deficit. But the United States is not a polity directed by Keynesian insights, theories, or values.

In the United States, the Democrats have tried, with decreasing conviction, to defend the legacy of New Deal and Great Society Keynesianism: Social Security, food stamps, the earned income tax credit, funding for college education, and similar measures all tend to the same purpose. These measures tend to bolster consumption, especially to the extent that they funnel resources to those with lower incomes. Second, Democratic valence issues tend to stabilize demand and diminish the impact of recession through programs designed to guarantee income, including the minimum wage, Social Security, proposed universal medical insurance, and so on. The traditional Republican attack on these programs is that they are irresponsible because we cannot afford them. The Democratic response has been to bolster up the defense of these programs by making sure that they are adequately funded and thus not irresponsible.

So the balanced budget religion of late nineteenth-century fiscal orthodoxy is not the same as the balanced budget advocacy in the early twenty-first-century United States. In the late nineteenth century, the goal of opponents of social welfare was principally to keep their own taxes down. They did this by opposing the expansion of the state. In the early twenty-first century, advocates of social welfare defend the principle of Keynesian redistribution by such fiscal orthodoxy as balanced budgets and paying down the national debt.

By contrast, the Republican Party remains the antitax party, with a vengeance. Keynesian principles are, when convenient, misappropriated to justify fiscal misconduct and tax-cutting that amounts to pillaging the Treasury. The driving goal of such politics appears identical to the short-term interests of corporations worried about their next quarterly report: the main thing is to pay off political support with tax cuts for the short-term gain of consolidating power. Whether this practice deliberately constrains the expansion of social programs, as has been suggested, is actually secondary to the immediate goal of making payoffs. The refund checks that have arrived for most taxpayers since President George W. Bush assumed office in 2001—$200 here, $400 there—are a bald-faced effort to induce in the middle-class taxpayer the same rapacity of spirit that motivates the corporate contributor. In short, can elections be bought by giving voters a few hundred dollars today in return for higher taxes and reduced services and reduced income security tomorrow?

Well, it would seem so. There is little doubt that in spite of razor-thin electoral results nationwide, the Republican Party, which today is fundamentally the party of the conservative South, has found an effective strategy for dominating American politics, with major repercussions domestically and worldwide. These repercussions will be not only political and social but also biospheric, as there is no evidence that the southern oligarchs have any commitment to mitigate the disastrous developments in the world's atmosphere, oceans, and forests.

Even if conservative strategy fails to eviscerate Social Security and other income redistribution programs, it does have the effect of forcing the defenders of Keynesian redistribution to raise taxes and balance the budget when (and if) they get back into office. This in turn guarantees the vilification of the party of redistribution at the hands of the party of no-taxation, which reinforces the solidarity of the antitax constituency whose worst fears are realized when fiscally orthodox Keynesians come into power and close the budget deficit in order to maintain the macroeconomically stabilizing mechanisms of income redistribution.

Thus Democrats remain Keynesians but are no longer advocates of deficit finance. Such sobriety cannot compete against the animus of pillage that motivates the corporate moguls of the Republican Party and the passel of fundamentalists and agricultural rent-seekers that they tow in their wake, on a platform of anti-Darwinism and antiabortion.

The Social Security Debate and the Emergence of Anti-Keynesian Political Leadership

> *We cannot, as a community, provide for future consumption by financial expedients but only by current physical output.*
> —Keynes, General Theory

The core program for Keynesian redistribution in the United States and most of the rest of the industrialized world is Social Security. Almost everywhere, we see this debate framed in terms of increasing private saving: that is, sending a signal to producers that their products are not needed. Yet it is the economic vigor of these producers that will create the future productive assets on which retirees will depend.

The Republican Party's desire to strangle government finance makes the public at large less secure about its own future. Though government bonds have been the litmus test of secure investment for decades, it is bruited about that Social Security faces imminent collapse. Individuals are made to feel that the same government that regularly pays interest on several trillion dollars of outstanding bonds is essentially broke, unable to meet its future commitments. Therefore a person planning for retirement must assume the worst, that there will be no social assistance forthcoming. Everyone must save maximally for retirement on the assumption that no income will be available from Social Security. If it is "every man for himself," then individuals are logically led to conclude that Social Security is a fraud, critically undermining not only the program's political support, but spurring millions to defer consumption and save for a perilous future. It follows directly from Keynes's analysis that scaring people into saving, as a public policy of official intimidation, is bound to have a negative impact on economic performance. Today's consumption and incomes will fall to the extent that the propaganda is taken seriously. The economic structure on which to build tomorrow's productivity will be weakened.

The incessant presentation of the image of a bankrupt Social Security system is a fraudulent scare tactic similar to that successfully employed against universal health care in the 1990s. At that time, people were frightened into thinking they would not be able to choose a doctor, when in fact 40 million people had no doctor at all. And now a generation is being raised on the lie that it cannot reasonably expect a payout from the retirement system to which it contributes.

In this debate, the U.S. tradition of mythic individualism comes together with traditional, non-Keynesian economics in an unusual way. Every individual senses the need to squirrel away money for retirement. The economic doctrine of "virtuous savings" adds to the individual's natural bias by saying that such saving is, macroeconomically, a rational policy.

However, Social Security is not a box into which contributors put money. It is a transfer program from those who work to those who do not. The doctrine of "virtuous savings" would have us believe that there is some other way to do things, that by investing in the private sector there will magically be more resources by which those who do not work will be supported by those who do. This implies that a private system would not face bankruptcy while a government system would, because, it is said, in the government system the ratio of people paying into the retirement system—the Social Security transfer system—becomes unworkable.

However, there is no way around the fact that whatever the economic arrangements, those who work must support those who are too old to work. Much of the panic literature on Social Security focuses on the "program dependency ratio," as vividly illustrated in the following sentence: "As recently as 1950, there were 16 workers for every Social Security beneficiary. Today there are only 3.3. By 2030, there will be fewer than two. The Social Security pyramid is unsustainable."[20]

Such alarming statements are not just bad Keynesianism, they are bad economics. After all, the dependency ratio for Social Security is only a proxy for the population of workers to retirees. Any way you cut the cake, the working must support the nonworking.[21] The nonworking must receive in some way goods and services from those who work. This is the fundamental "ratio problem" that cannot be wished away, and it must instantly make us suspect that the true motivation for the attack on Social Security is a cold, calculated attempt to destroy one of the most successful income stabilization and redistributive antipoverty programs in history.

The forecast of a fall from 3.3 : 1 to 2 : 1 is a mere 30 percent reduction in the support ratio, whereas the fall from 16 : 1 to 3.3 : 1, from the 1950s to the present, is itself a reduction nearly thrice as great, of 79 percent, and it occurred in decades of lower productivity. Yet today's ratio, which surely would have seemed an extravagance in the 1930s when Social Security was first enacted, has been shouldered rather easily. It would take a much less dramatic increase in productivity than we have had in previous decades to obviate any supposed future Social Security crisis. Indeed, in the 1990s, in spite of tens of millions of Social Security annuitants, the government accumulated a surplus. A 1 percent per annum growth in productivity will compound to 34 percent over thirty years, at which point it is no longer a fantasy to see two workers supporting one retiree.

The only real issue is the political one, the willingness to redistribute increased levels of income. The Social Security trustees actually use a very conservative assumption of 1.5 percent annual productivity growth. While the historical post–World War II average of annual productivity growth rates was in fact higher (2.48 percent), the real issue again hinges on income distribution.[22] If in the next decades the aggregate income of productivity growth is primarily captured by the upper quintile of earners whose contributions to the fund are capped, then the fund will be bankrupt. If productivity growth were instead directed at furthering consumption (gains being captured by the lower-income quintiles), a not incidental effect would be an increase of funds into the Social Security system. Thus the real Social Security "crisis" is caused by the class structure of the United States and the violent antipathy of the right wing to any form of income redistribution, including remedies to the unequal wage structure.

Conceding, for argument, that the declining ratio of contributors to recipients is a pressing problem, we must now ask whether the mechanism of private savings actually constitutes a reasonable alternative to a "pay as you go" Social Security system. Private savings will be invested in government bonds—funded by taxpayers who work. They will also be invested in corporate bonds, funded by companies that receive income from purchases, purchases predicated on the direct and transferred incomes of those who work. Finally, retirement income will also be drawn from stocks, whose value will reflect the earnings capabilities of the companies that depend upon the aggregate purchasing power of those who work.

Conversion to a privatized system means a huge surge in private demand for investment assets such as stocks and bonds. This implies, among other things, a rise in their prices. The working population of the future, instead of facing a higher Social Security tax for transfer payments, will instead have to put more of its own money aside for retirement. That is because workers saving for retirement will have to pay more for higher-priced stocks whose dividends and potential appreciation ratios will be lower. A broadly increased demand for public and private bond ownership would also have the effect of lowering the effective interest rate, meaning that the return on bonds would be lower. So future workers would need to buy more of them. Workers will pay more out and get less back.

Under lower effective interest rates, the economy would have that much more stimulus; that would be a neoclassical view, and a possible reply to the argument just given. The Keynesian response is that the increased emphasis on private savings will have two negative effects. First, consumers will be encouraged to buy more financial assets, at higher prices, and fewer real goods. This can only mean a contraction of effective demand and a drag on the output of the economy as a whole, meaning, among other things, more unemployment: income will contract as saving increases. Arguably, this saving will be equivalent to today's "forced saving" (really income transfer) in the existing Social Security program. But since the returns on private investments will be uncertain, cautious savers will need to make a greater provision than they would under a government system.

There is also a real potential calamity in extremely low interest rates caused by "excess demands" for bonds: a structural flirtation, induced by the privatized retirement system, with the liquidity trap discussed by Keynes (*General Theory* 1964, 202), as presented in Professor Ventelou's book.

Privatized retirement savings will also put the considerable purchasing power of retirees into instruments whose value changes on a daily, even minute-by-minute, basis. Retirees would have to consider their pool of retirement funds and plan conservatively against a fall in asset prices, which will diminish aggregate income in itself, and when those declines in asset prices occur, retirees will hoard their principal even more tightly, further depressing spending, income, and, obviously, asset prices. Thus, private retirement funds are procyclical: they make downturns worse.

A government-funded Social Security is countercyclical. That is, retirees receive the same amount from the government on a monthly basis regardless of whether the economy is doing well or poorly. That is the nature of the government's guarantee. What it means is that seniors can rationally calculate their spending as a percentage of income. It also means that the market for goods and services will be steadied, adding certainty to the calculations of employers and thereby stabilizing the climate for investment and for jobs.

These are by themselves compelling reasons not to leap from a government program to a private one. Nonetheless, there is yet another fallacy that is trumpeted: privatized retirement funds are better because they will "outperform" a government program.

One of the most popular ways to attack Social Security is to compare individuals' rate of return on the money they put aside for Social Security as opposed to the historic rate of return on privately held assets, which are estimated through the use of historical averages that are then projected into the future. When this is done, it is said, privately invested money does better.[23]

What this approach neglects is that the rate of return on privately held investments reflects the fact that we have had Social Security for seventy years. There are no data about what the economy would look like without the tremendous stabilizing force of the Social Security and other transfer programs, such as unemployment insurance. Or, more accurately, such data as we do have date from before World War II, and the terms we use for that sort of social policy include "Great Depression" and the periodic, "busts" that characterized the nineteenth century. These phrases are pointed reminders that a capitalist economy without income stabilization is—unstable. It is pointless to compare the post–World War II return on private investments as an alternative to Social Security when the performance of those investments is not, as economists would say, "an independent variable," independent of the existence of the Social Security program itself. Assets perform well because the economy performs well, and the economy performs well, among other reasons, because it has a large Social Security program.[24]

The whole theory of antitax economics is, in fact, that the economic and technical development of the past seventy years has occurred in spite of, not because of, the government's management of income flows within the economy. These arguments have an almost hallucinatory quality. Everything Keynes has to teach us about the unreliability of the stock and bond markets as mechanisms to provide investment and prosperity says that we tamper with Social Security arrangements at our peril. The advocates of Social Security privatization are making a multitrillion dollar wager that Keynes was wrong and that the economic performance of the national economy for the past seventy years has had nothing to do with the stabilizing impact of income transfers to the old. The economic approaches that excoriate taxation and view all forms of redistribution as evil are faced with a mind-boggling paradox: that the richest, most technologically advanced, and most stable societies in world history have somehow bumbled their way into economic prosperity in spite of, not because of, the transfer programs in place.

Comparing the macroeconomic Social Security program to another macroeconomic program, the institutional controls over the interest rate through the Federal Reserve, makes the point as well. A high interest rate discourages borrowing; under most conditions, it leads to higher unemployment. The cost of fighting inflation can be calculated in terms of lost incomes, lost tax revenues, and higher interest payments; one can even calculate the number of homes that are not built. But the true social cost, leaving aside the very real social and psychological impacts of unemployment, must also include the technologies whose development is forgone or delayed because a higher priority is placed on preserving the purchasing power of the currency. The crude quantification of lost income and output is a very poor indicator of the true cost of a policy of high interest rates.[25]

Similarly, a crude calculation of the individual benefits from Social Security on a paid-in, paid-out basis grossly distorts the purpose of the program. What each person should be asked to quantify is not his or her anticipated rate of personal return, but what each might be willing to pay, as a matter of social policy, not to endure crises on a par with the 1930s or 1890s, much less the more transient but real fears of crises such as those in 1907 and 1920. The answer is that if protection from a society ravaged by these crises is what you get in exchange for your Social Security contribution, and on top of that you actually get your money back when you are old, you have a bargain. Each new generation "gets" out of Social Security the technologies and productive economy developed by the generation now retired. That is not a bad thing to pay for.

These things said, we must now ask why the Keynesian innovations of the New Deal and the Great Society are under such sustained attack in the United States. There are two underlying causes, the first in the historic political structure of the United States, the second in its economic transformation since the end of World War II.

For a century after the Civil War, the free trade South stayed with the Democratic Party. Beginning with the Wilson administration and continuing through the Roosevelt administration up to Johnson's presidency, the progressive side of the Democratic Party had an ongoing "deal with the devil." The southern wing was intrinsically hostile to labor rights, unions, civil rights, and redistributive policies that had strong support in the Democratic Party's Midwest and Northeast urban bastions. But the South would deliver a congressional majority to the Democratic Party, because of the party's support for free trade, so long as it received some shelter from the redistributive intentions of the New Deal. The shameful second tier minimum wage for agricultural workers is one example. And of course, the second shameful deal was on civil rights for blacks, whose plight was ignored, even though another major domain of civil rights—workers' rights—received a great deal of attention.

Agricultural regions in general benefited little from most of the classic New Deal programs. Social policy treats farmers as small business owners, not wage earners, and they act as small business owners: they underreport income where possible and as a result cannot expect much by way of Social Security benefits. Similarly, unemployment insurance and other protections have little appeal for farmers as business owners.

Viewing today's farms as "industrial agriculture" does little to suggest a business constituency for Keynesianism. The biggest appeal of Keynesian stimulus, its textbook formulation, is that increased demand will lead to more orders for factory goods. But of course consumption of food cannot respond very directly to such stimulus, except in the case of those who are literally starving; for the rest, increased income shifts preferences from one kind of food, such as grain, to a more expensive one, such as meat. In fact, the biggest political priority of the agricultural sector is not for redistribution but for access to foreign markets, the fastest way to increase aggregate demand. The repeated, decades-old clashes over American entry into Europe's agricultural markets and the politics of grain exports to the former Soviet Union show where the agricultural sector's highest political priorities are.

The farm sector responds atypically—assuming manufacturers are typical—to economic crisis. Farmers tend to overproduce in economic hard times, in a desperate bid to keep income level as per unit prices fall. Especially if they are self-employed, they cannot gain anything by layoffs, and the equivalent of shutting down the factory to a farmer means losing the family home. Massive overproduction is a symptom of depression in the farm sector. A stimulus that increases demand in order to increase consumption, in the textbook phrase, finds its opposite in the agricultural sector, where an economic recovery brings about higher prices and decreases in production (and incidentally better conservation practices) as income stabilizes. Moreover, in agriculture, many of the more durable commodities, such as tobacco, cotton, and grain, experience a large hangover effect. Even with government purchase of stocks, overproduction in crisis years will continue to cast a cloud of unsold, accumulated inventory on current farm crops as the economy recovers.

The kinds of support that farmers require, in fact, generally run to production controls and price guarantees, really more of a government-sponsored cartelization and system of price supports than anything like the income redistribution that creates demand. Indeed, government revenue spent on income redistribution is, by definition, tax revenue not made available for agricultural price supports. And it is price supports that are of far more consequence to farmers. Thus, the New Deal, in addition to the minimum wage and Social Security, also brought with it programs such as the tobacco and peanut quotas, which met the income stabilization needs of the Deep South's larger farmers, while at the same time protecting them from increased costs by deliberately relegating agricultural labor to second-class status. Social Security was, of course, a huge boon to many poor workers in the South, even when based on their rock-bottom wage levels. Nonetheless, it was agricultural support programs that purchased southern elites' acquiescence to a more progressive agenda for the industrial parts of the country.

If we look at the U.S. electoral map today, we might say that the Republicans get their core votes in the countryside and move from that base *in* to the suburbs, whereas Democrats get their core votes in the cities and move from that base *out* to the suburbs. Elections are decided by who makes the best case for the suburban vote. The presidential election of 2000 clearly showed that the core support for the modern Republican Party, dominated by southern leadership, is the southern and midwestern agricultural states. This is not to say it is a party of farmers, and today even rural constituents are clamoring for prescription drug coverage and are protective of Social Security. But the Republicans have inherited, on the whole, a southern party with a rural social base that did not get a great deal of attention from New Deal progressivism.

Today, the much diminished redistributive or New Deal coalition is concentrated in the Northeast and on the West Coast, where minority constituencies continue to push for redistribution (in whatever form, including schools and medical access) while the well-educated suburbanites struggle, against the tide, to preserve a commitment to ecological sanity.

This regional factionalism helps explain the faltering national political commitment to the principle of redistribution. The rural areas that are the now Republican stronghold were never the favored constituencies of the New Deal, and core values of these regions were actively attacked both by the politics and economics of the Great Society and by the cultural mores—and especially the racial integration—of the 1960s. The Democrats cannot win a majority in the post-1994 House of Representatives because their votes are not efficiently distributed, causing them to win by large margins in the districts where they win, and lose by smaller margins in the large number of districts where they lose. This pattern reflects not just the historic concentrations of the black vote but the tendency of immigrant populations, a natural base for favoring redistributive social policies, to cluster together in urban immigrant communities. In essence, demographic changes, coupled with the flight of southern reactionaries from the Democratic Party, have turned the South, and to a lesser extent the Midwest, into the core base of the anti–New Deal.

In the suburbs we see a different phenomenon. The middle class no longer depends on industrial unionized wages. The impact of stimulus measures on the jobs of lawyers, teachers, and software workers is bound to be much less direct than it is for industrial workers. Industrial workers more easily make the connection between the unit output of their factories, their job security, and the state of the economy. But not only is industrial production shifting overseas, but the number of jobs industry supplies is falling worldwide in absolute terms, following Marx's hoary but useful prediction that the increasing "organic composition of capital" (capital intensiveness) would shift toward ever more efficient mechanized production.[26]

Indeed, as industrial production has shifted overseas—or diminished in absolute terms—and the locus of American unionization has shifted to workers on government payrolls, the character of American politics takes on a tone of massive assault against the principle of government itself. The last bastion of unionism is that segment of the population that works for the state and federal governments; and in fact, this is the last segment of secure jobs in today's economy—though the current crisis in state finance may diminish this, too. The plutocracy, on the other hand, conscious of how much it stands to gain by reducing its own tax burden, has no qualms about using massive campaign funds to whip the insecure portion of the population into a frenzy of resentment against the economic security and privileges (medical insurance and retirement savings being seen as "privileges" and not rights in the American polity) that characterize the diminishing and increasingly public unionized sector.

Finally, the immediate benefit of "industrial stimulus" in the textbook Keynesian formulation are now only partially shared by American workers; the rest go to the factories of Japan and sweatshops and prison camps of China. Among the educated professionals who are in the private sector and support the Democratic Party, there may be more to gain in the short term from the government's commitment to extending overseas property rights (entertainment, software, scientific patents) than from any direct stimulus to their business by a government commitment to fiscal deficits or redistribution. The Clinton administration's emphasis on intellectual property rights, combined with a commitment to some redistribution (earned income tax credit) and balanced budgets, says much about the new realities that govern the macroeconomy and its political tendencies.

To be blunt, at this time there appears to be no significant natural constituency for Keynesian redistributive policies in the United States, other than the urban poor.[27] And as for deficits as a means to boost industrial production, they benefit an increasingly smaller constituency in the United States, having only indirect and difficult-to-measure impacts on the agricultural and professional service sectors. In this sense, the collapse of the Democrats and with them the New Deal is as much a reflection of a shift in the character and distribution of the "forces of production" as it is of the intense divide, itself reminiscent of nineteenth-century regional factionalism, that evolved out of the Johnson era's Great Society progressivism.

Of course, the Democrats, during their fifty-year ascendancy in Congress, did not effectively deal with the medical insurance issue: so much the worse for them. The main reason is that during this time the Democratic Party was the home of the socially reactionary southern conservatives who now rule the Republican Party. True progressive bursts had to await those moments when Democratic majorities were so big (usually 260 or so seats out of 435) that the southern faction could be ignored. At other times, as during Ronald Reagan's first term, the Ninety-seventh Congress (1981–1982) proved particularly toxic, due to the collaboration of southern Democrats with the Republican "minority." The Ninety-seventh Congress, in fact, was an anticipation of the Republican Congresses of the 1990s that shut down government, impeached President Clinton, and continue to run amok in our new century. The de facto majority of conservative southern Democrats and Republicans initiated, among other things, the first tax revolt of the rich at the federal level and the huge deficits that followed.

So for the past fifty years we have not had a true "Labor Party" in the United States, so much as we have had a labor party that failed in its struggle against the poison pill of its southern delegates. These are best described as America's trash Junkers, embodying all of that nineteenth-century German group's social conservatism and militarism, but entirely lacking its intelligence, culture, and wit. We can only speculate what a Democratic Party stripped of its southern conservative burden would do if it actually commanded a stable majority in Congress. We are not, however, likely to find out in the near future.

Environmental Politics

> *I conclude that the duty of ordering the current volume of investment cannot safely be left in private hands.*
> —Keynes, General Theory

It appears from the preceding section that Keynesian economics is uprooted from any natural contemporary political base. That does not mean its analytic foundations are wrong. It does mean that no one has come up with an effective way to package Keynes's insights in our own era and that, as a consequence, progressive politics operates without a coherent core of economic and social values. As a result, progressive politics, and the Keynesian view of managing capitalism, are everywhere on the defensive.

The American right, at its heart, subscribes to the theory of the night watchman state, which sees the proper role of the government as providing for national defense in the foreign arena and securing property rights in the domestic one. With about 2.1 million prisoners, the United States maintains nearly 20 percent of the world's prison population, and its military budget exceeds those of the next ten nations combined. The invasion of Iraq and the jailing of the domestic population are "legitimate expenditures" according to the theory of the night watchman state. Investment in a costly infrastructure for the production and distribution of alternative fuels, or reducing air and water pollution, are not.

There is an unfortunate confusion on this score between neoclassical economics as it is preached as a political ideology, and neoclassical economics as it is. Neoclassical economics is not intrinsically hostile to environmental regulation. The theory of negative externalities asks us, perhaps too simplistically, to put a dollar value on the harm caused by pollution and other harmful activities in order to price products more accurately in terms of their true social as well as private costs of production. Such exercises in "externality pricing" are not intrinsically hostile to a Keynesian approach to the environment.

Nonetheless, in a polity characterized by the increasingly potent religion of the night watchman state, any state-sponsored investment is seen as a drag on the economy: whether the government goes into a toxic landfill and cleans it up, a direct investment in environmental quality, or whether it requires polluting utilities in the Midwest to install better emission controls, a government-mandated investment, both are seen as illegitimate uses of state power. And these relatively simple and pragmatic exercises in the exercise of state power pale compared to the genuine level of need, such as, for example, the rapid development of fuel cell vehicles and subsidized construction of a distribution network to meet the needs of these new vehicles.

In the neoclassical view, any mandated expenditure not directly dictated by the market is seen as threatening profits, the incentive to invest, and therefore employment. But even so, neoclassical economics cannot be said to condone ignoring the environment, because the theory of externalities says that there is in fact a true cost to be paid, and that it will be paid, even if it does not get captured in the price of a good. It is paid in the harm suffered by the general public. In the hands of the American political right, the latter point is lost; emphasizing only the putative loss of employment and profits, the doctrine gets simplified into a general attack on the legitimacy of any government involvement in the rational direction of investment expenditure, no matter how necessary. Yet nothing in the theory of democratic governance says that a people's representatives should not vote to acquire, on behalf of the public, an environmental good instead of some private good. After all, roads and weapons for armies are public goods, and if a polity should wish to acquire clean air or take some protective measures against the green-house effect, that is within reason as both a political and an economic objective. In today's political climate, the desire to invest on behalf of public goods such as the environment is seen as an idiotic romanticism of no conceivable relevance to the real world. Yet there is every reason to suppose that the public might prefer to spend its collective wealth on a collective environmental improvement rather than leave the private sector with the resources it needs to develop a new flavor of potato chip.

Regrettably, too, the failure to keep a Keynesian perspective in the forefront of contemporary debates gets in the way of understanding just what it is that happens when the government mandates environmental regulation. Invariably, when an environmental problem is identified, the cost of the fix is calculated, added to the production cost of the product that is causing a problem, and then shown to be too expensive for reasonable consumers to bear.

For example, in the 1950s and 1960s, the automotive industry put up as much opposition to catalytic converters to control smog as today a large number of industries are putting up against any form of carbon dioxide or other greenhouse gas reductions. The form of the argument is the same, calling for more studies and underlining the huge impact on consumers of addressing this problem.

Keynes teaches us that unemployment is a function of deficient investment. The simplest way to interpret this statement is that wherever unemployment appears it is surely a sign that investment is falling. Many of the traditional Keynesian policies have sought either to bolster demand or to substitute government investment (such as in roads or housing) for deficient private investment.

But there is another category of investment that stems from regulation. We might say that every firm has a certain underutilized ability to invest that stems from the natural timorousness of corporate decision makers. No one in an industry can say with certainty at what price all produced goods will "clear." Since firms do not want to undertake expensive and profitless investment, it is rational for the five dominant firms in an industry to target perhaps 90 percent of total anticipated production and let minor firms take the rest, on the theory that if sales prove to be only 93 percent of what had been anticipated earlier, the major firms will not have stuck their necks out in a risky quest to dominate 100 percent of anticipated sales.

When we impose uniform regulations on an industry, we force it to invest in itself above the level that the individual prudence of firms, either alone or as an aggregate, would have permitted. This act of mandated investment boosts aggregate income of the nation as a whole, and rarely does it force a firm into bankruptcy. Environmental costs are typically discussed as "negative externality costs" that are not reflected in the price. But paying to reduce externality costs is no different from purchasing other forms of public goods. Roads, schools, and pollution controls are among the many expenses that must be paid if capitalism is to exist at all. Expenditure dictated by regulation is no different from taxation in its essence. Both have the potential to boost aggregate spending and spur the economy.

This is, in fact, why the civilized world is what it is and has lasted as long as it has. To judge from the battalions of lobbyists maintained by industry, each act of taxation, raising the minimum wage, or protecting the environment threatens the end of capitalism. Were that true, Madagascar and similar regions with low levels of social protection, wages, and taxation would be capitalism's paradise. In fact, capitalism survives because of, not in spite of, these collective expenditures.

The automobile catalytic converter exemplifies all these points. The approximately $300 per vehicle cost of the catalytic converter has allowed California to grow from a population of 10 million in the 1960s to 30 million today. The state would have been uninhabitable had automobiles continued to spew pollution at the same rate as they did in the 1950s. It is fair to say, therefore, that the hundreds of billions of dollars in increased real estate value, the numerous businesses, the aviation and entertainment industries in southern California, the Silicon Valley businesses in the northern part of the state, the continued viability of the state's billion-dollar agriculture, are all predicated on the control of automobile pollution. Had vehicle pollution not been controlled, creative and well-educated people would have fled. The "return on investment" on the catalytic converter is thus fundamentally incalculable, but were someone to try, it would surely run into thousands of dollars returned for every dollar spent.

Yet the entire political debate on vehicle pollution has always been framed in terms of the cost of the installation per vehicle and its effect on individual consumers' willingness to purchase a new car.

The catalytic converter suggests other lessons relevant to a Keynesian perspective. Traditionally, we think of depletable resources as obeying some kind of iron law of finitude. A modern Keynesian approach would lead us to thinking of many, if not all, of these problems as responsive to increased investment. The finite supply of air in California saturated easily at 1950s levels of automobile emissions, but was effectively increased a hundredfold by the catalytic converter.

Certain problems, of course, respond more to the right investment rather than to investment as such. Depleted fish stocks worldwide may not easily recover even with any foreseeable capital investment. But if the problem is phrased in terms of providing suitable animal or nonanimal proteins for the human diet, there are many alternatives. And the fact that public preference has been conditioned to certain foods by custom and advertising is simply another question of investment—this time in changing customs.

Investment, is, therefore, properly seen as a function of political power. The total level of investment and the direction of investment are amenable to political controls, and, moreover, the capitalist economy can perform well because of them. It can perform better, in fact, than it is likely to perform if left to its own devices. We need only consider what would have become of California, and much of the rest of the United States' urban areas, had the Detroit automakers not been forced to spend to clean up the automobile.

A final shibboleth of the right-wing approach to environmental regulation is that "we can't afford it." President Bush said as much in justifying the United States's failure to adhere to the Kyoto protocols for controlling the greenhouse effect. With unemployment rising and profits falling, the argument goes, businesses cannot afford the burden of investments needed to control the emissions that may alter the entire planetary environment in very short order.

From a Keynesian perspective, this claim is very troubling. When the economy is at full employment, the claim that we cannot afford environmental pollution controls makes at least superficial sense. Under full employment, entrepreneurs have collectively found a use for virtually everyone. If we decide to do something about the environment under conditions of full employment, the workers who do good environmental work must be hired away from the firms that already are using them. This implies, among other things, rising wage costs and a diversion of resources from the private sector's priorities.

Under conditions of less than full employment, however, precisely when neoclassical theory tells us that "firms are weak," we have, in fact, surplus labor. With many thousands of engineers and software experts now out of work, we have a talented pool of people, desperate for income, whose collective skills could surely be put to use to make the economy more energy-efficient and thus do something about the greenhouse effect. This could be done without bidding up wages and diverting labor resources from firms that have already made the judgment that in the current market they do not want or need these workers.

This reasoning also applies to physical goods. Under full employment conditions, every factor input is being produced so far as workers can be found to produce it. So if, for example, building fuel cells requires new metal alloys, under full employment the resources to make the new alloys would have to be bid away from other buyers who prefer that those resources be kept focused on other metals for other uses. But when the economy is weaker, the public's demand for "greener" transportation and the new alloys that will help provide it does not have to compete directly against traditional supplies for traditional markets. Firms have unutilized productive capacity to divert to new types of demand.

An appreciation of the Keynesian facts of life is, indeed, essential to give a sound rationale for the pursuit of environmental policies under capitalism. Keynes's observation that "the duty of ordering the current volume of investment cannot safely be left in private hands" (*General Theory* 1964, 320) is nowhere more evident today than in environmental policy. Public investment or, at the least, publicly mandated investment is essential if we are to face the ecological challenges of our time.

But a final point is this, that under the theory of negative externalities there is, as I have said above, no way around the fact that costs are being paid by society for the production of harmful goods. A liberal neoclassical approach would say that we need to address such problems regardless of whether the economy is at full or less than full employment, and a Keynesian liberal would have to say the same. The Keynesian would simply point out that under the conditions of less than full employment, the impact of environmental spending mandates is less than that implied by neoclassical assumptions. Regulation and mandates actually furnish an opportunity to increase society's total output of goods and services in a particularly socially useful manner, and for Keynesians there is no bidding away of resources for productive investment. A neoclassical approach has a hard time with this argument, typically seeing in unemployment a failure of wages to adjust to the price that would allow for full employment equilibrium, and in the increased costs of regulation an incremental disincentive to invest.

Keynesian and neoclassical assumptions both lead to the conclusion that, under full employment conditions, reducing environmental negative externalities would, in fact, bid resources away from alternative investments. The politics of the American right give us neither informed neoclassicism, which at a minimum delivers the bad news that the price of environmental degradation must be paid, nor progressive Keynesianism. We get, instead, unmitigated spoliation.

Conclusion

> *Whilst, therefore, the enlargement of the functions of government, involved in the task of adjusting one to another the propensity to consume and the inducement to invest, would seem to a nineteenth-century publicist or to a contemporary American financier to be a terrific encroachment on individualism, I defend it, on the contrary, both as the only practicable means of avoiding the destruction of existing economic forms in their entirety and as the condition of the successful functioning of individual initiative.*
> —Keynes, General Theory

Keynes tells us that a capitalist society depends on a class of investors whose irrationality makes them uniquely unsuited for the full utilization of productive resources and, just as importantly, for the provision of such public goods as are desperately needed by the majority of people. Keynes was fond of mentioning housing in the *General Theory*, but this is shorthand for public goods, and we may add public health care, education, and environmental quality to the list.

Keynes famously called for the "euthanasia of the rentier" and the "socialization of investment" (*General Theory* 1964, 320, 376). He was himself a rentier and he certainly was no revolutionary. Nonetheless, his approach suggests an underlying political assessment about the ability of capitalists to behave rationally, not just economically, but at any level. Keynes focused on the behavior of investors in the strictest sense, as abstract market participants. His theory did not extend to how these market participants would impact the political process that affects the government's decision making.

With the repudiation of the Kyoto protocols, the new venture into world imperialism, growing income inequality, a skyrocketing federal debt whose only purpose is to exacerbate income inequality, debt reforms designed to harass the poor, and the fiscal bankruptcy of the American state governments, we are on the road to a lower quality of life. It is greatly to be feared that, short of some monumental political reversal, the United States will become a giant version of the Philippines or some other third-world country. Keynes's austere wit and brilliant criticisms directly targeted the robber baron mentality that today is presented as the key to wealth and prosperity. But the spirit of rapacity is running wild and every day seems to grow more omnipotent. Under an incessant barrage of propaganda from the right, the United States has become a nation of somnambulists who have forgotten the time when an American president could say, as Roosevelt did at his second inaugural in 1937, "We have always known that heedless self-interest was bad morals; we know now that it is bad economics."

Unfortunately, however, the ground today may not be fertile for the concept of enlightened self-interest and that is at the core of Keynesian attitudes to the management of a capitalist polity. The acerbic criticism of Keynesians by Paul Sweezy comes to mind (*Theory of Capitalist Development*, 348–349):

> [V]arious proposals for liberal capitalist reform . . . have been put forward in recent years. It is sufficient to point out that those which deserve to be taken seriously derive more or less directly from the writings of John Maynard Keynes and that their basis idea in every case is social control over consumption and investment. Generally speaking their logical consistency cannot be challenged, either on their own ground or on the basis of the Marxian analysis of the reproduction process. The critique of Keynesian theories of liberal capitalist reform starts, therefore, not from their economic logic but rather from their faulty (usually implicit) assumptions about the relationship, or perhaps one should say lack of relationship, between economics and political action. The Keynesians tear the economic system out of its social context and treat it as though it were a machine to be sent to the repair shop there to be overhauled by an engineer state.[28]

Professor Ventelou's useful book, which is now available to English-speaking audiences, is an exercise in optimism. If, as Sweezy indicates, the "logical consistency" of the Keynesian approach "cannot be challenged," then it is worth reflecting on what is *useful*. There is much to render one pessimistic in the current political environment. But optimism is one of the better fuels for political action; it needs no justification but is by itself a resource. There is no sin in exploiting the insights of a theory that not only has explanatory validity but that promises to address challenges of dismaying dimensions.

Indeed, Sweezy's dislike of reformism notwithstanding, it is pretty clear that the only effective challenge to the dominant spirit of rapacity lies in a Keynesian liberal internationalism, which alone promises to face the instabilities of capital markets and fluctuating currencies, as well as the increasing inequalities of skewed income distributions. Either the collective challenges facing contemporary capitalism will be addressed with Keynesian insights within the context of current democratic structures, or they will not be addressed at all. Or, more accurately, we can say that such solutions to pressing ecological and social problems as may become policy, absent Keynesianism and democracy, are likely to reflect an extreme crisis. The accompanying political upheaval and exact nature of such a crisis can, at this time, remain only speculative.

Readers of Professor Ventelou's book will acquire a solid foundation for understanding Keynes's work generally and especially his magnificent *General Theory of Employment, Interest, and Money*. The *General Theory* is, in its intention, depth of insight, and austere execution, one of the great works of Western civilization. It is a marvelous gift from the otherwise barbarous and lugubrious decade in which it was written. Professor Ventelou's work opens the door to understanding that great work and offers a hopeful view of the benefits of adapting Keynes's ideas to the crises of our own time.

Notes

1. John M. Keynes, "The Economic Consequences of the Peace" in *Collected Writings of John Maynard Keynes*, vol. 2. (Cambridge: Macmillan St. Martin's Press for The Royal Economic Society, 1971; first published 1919).

2. Adam Smith, *An Inquiry into the Nature and Causes of the Wealth of Nations*, 2 vols. (Chicago: University of Chicago Press, 1976; first published 1776).

3. Immanuel Kant, *Perpetual Peace: A Philosophical Essay* (London: S. Sonnenschein, 1903; first published 1795).

4. John M. Keynes, *The General Theory of Employment, Interest, and Money* (New York: Harcourt Brace Jovanovich, 1964; first published 1936).

5. Modern apostles of "natural capitalism" actually espouse a Smithian view of

an innate or teleological drive to capitalism. Examples include Hernando de Soto's *The Mystery of Capital: Why Capitalism Triumphs in the West and Fails Everywhere Else* (New York: Basic Books, 2000) and Thomas Friedman's *The Lexus and the Olive Tree* (New York: Farrar, Strauss, and Giroux, 1999). Max Weber demolished Smith's premises, and by implication those of his followers, in *The Agrarian Sociology of Ancient Civilizations* (New York: Verso, 1976; first published in 1896). But Weber had the disadvantage of never having made the *New York Times* best-seller list.

6. A view explored recently by Bruce Russet and John R. O'Neal in *Triangulating Peace: Democracy, Interdependence, and International Organizations* (New York: W.W. Norton, 2001).

7. And also consistent with nightmarish views of a belligerent world order, such as John Mearsheimer's *The Tragedy of Great Power Politics* (New York: W.W. Norton, 2001).

8. See, for example, George N. Hatsopoulos, Paul R. Krugman, and Lawrence H. Summers, "U.S. Competitiveness: Beyond the Trade Deficit," *Science* 241, 1988, 299–307; and Lawrence H. Summers, Chris Carroll, and Alan S. Blinder, "Why Is U.S. National Saving So Low?" *Brookings Papers on Economic Activity 1987*, no. 2, 1987, 607–642.

9. Keynes, *Economic Consequences of the Peace*, 19.

10. See, for example, J.A. Hobson's *Imperialism: A Study* (Ann Arbor: University of Michigan Press, 1965; first published 1902). In Chapter 23 of the *General Theory*, Keynes gives a longer lineage, going back to Mandeville's incisive eighteenth-century economic poetry (pp. 359–361).

11. An excellent historical analysis of the evolution of applied Keynesianism from redistribution to tax cuts for businesses and the wealthy may be found in Robert Collins's *The Business Response to Keynes, 1929–1964* (New York: Columbia University Press, 1981).

12. See Randall Bartlett, *Economic Foundations of Political Power* (New York: Macmillan, 1973), for a rather sobering rational actor model of why this must be so.

13. See, for example, Paul M. Sweezy, *The Theory of Capitalist Development* (New York: Modern Reader Paperbacks, 1970; first edition 1942). Of special interest are pp. 348–350. See also pp. 62–63, 123–124 in Paul Baran's *Political Economy of Growth* (New York: Modern Reader Paperbacks, 1957).

14. See footnote 10, above.

15. Lynn Turgeon's pro-Keynesian arguments that see Nazi finance as successful unemployment policy in the 1930s do little to dispel, and inadvertently much to reinforce, the Marxist critique. See Turgeon's *Bastard Keynesianism: The Evolution of Economic Thinking and Policymaking since World War II* (Westport, CT: Greenwood Press, 1996).

16. Mark Harrison, "Resource Mobilization for World War II: The U.S.A., U.K., U.S.S.R., and Germany, 1938–1945," *Economic History Review*, n.s., 41, no. 2 (May 1988): 171–192.

17. A further oversimplification is that if deficit spending is necessarily Keynesian, balanced budgets must be non-Keynesian. In "Multiplier Effects of a Balanced Budget," *Econometrica* 13, no. 4 (October 1945): 311–318, Trygve Haavelmo advanced the thesis that when government taxes revenue and spends "at unity"—everything it has taken in—the stimulation to the economy is greater than if left in the hands of

taxpayers who save a percentage of their income (marginal propensity to consume less than unity). This implies among other things a greater social benefit to taxation on the incomes of the rich as opposed to the poor, though current social policy is going in the opposite direction. Haavelmo's thesis also means that the balanced budget coupled with progressive taxation is in fact Keynesian. It remains the case, however, that budget surpluses decrease aggregate income and are only logical as an anti-inflation measure under conditions of full employment.

18. Income and other economic data in this paragraph and the one that follows are from John M. Anderson, "The Wealth of U.S. Families: Analysis of Recent Census Data," Paper No. 233, November 10, 1999, U.S. Department of Commerce, Bureau of the Census (Chevy Chase, MD: Capital Research Associates); and Michael E. Davern and Patricia J. Fisher, "Household Net Worth and Asset Ownership, 1995," Bureau of the Census, Current Population Reports, Household Economic Studies, P70–71 (Washington, DC: U.S. Government Printing Office, 2001).

19. The welfare debate in the United States differs little from the nineteenth-century themes found in Karl Polanyi's *The Great Transformation: The Political and Economic Origins of Our Time* (Boston: Beacon Press, 1944). Keynes's theses about income distribution and the inherent volatility of investment fit very well with this book, which perhaps comes closer than any other to articulating a "Keynesian theory" of capitalist history.

20. Michael Tanner, "Social Security Is Sicker Than Some Politicians Believe," *Daily Commentary*, Washington, DC: Cato Institute, January 3, 1997, www.cato.org/dailys/1–03–97.html.

21. Andrew G. Biggs, in *Social Security: Is It "A Crisis That Doesn't Exist?"* SSP No. 221, Washington, DC: Cato Institute, October 5, 2000, argues that today we have 154 million workers and 38 million retirees and that by 2050 we will have only 186 million workers supporting 78 million retirees. Leaving aside the sheer weirdness of making assumptions about the economic structure of 2050—should Roosevelt have based policy in 1936 on anticipated conditions in 1986?—this author again fails to see the obvious point, that the ratio of workers to nonworkers is a fact of life. The claims exercised by privately held assets on the output of those 186 million workers will be a good deal more unstable than the claims exercised by the body politic.

22. Bureau of Labor Statistics, "Major Sector Productivity and Costs Index," PRS85006092, http://data.bls.gov. An indexed productivity series ("Major Sector Productivity and Costs Index: Business: Output: index, 1992 = 100, www.economagic.com/em-cgi/data.exe/blspr/prs84006043) shows the 1948–2002 compound productivity growth rate to be 3.5 percent.

23. There is even an Internet site (www.mysocialsecurity.org) where one can put in one's age and income and see how much one "loses" by contributing to Social Security versus what one would gain in a private fund. See Liqun Liu, Andrew J. Rettenmaier, and Zijun Wang, "Social Security and Market Risk," Policy Report No. 244, July 2001, College Station, TX: Private Enterprise Research Center, Texas A&M University. Other researchers tend to envision less drastic forms of privatization, with accounts under various degrees of government control. See, for example, Edward M. Gramlich, "Different Approaches for Dealing with Social Security," *American Economic Review* 86, no. 2, Papers and Proceedings of the Hundred and Eighth Annual Meeting of the American Economic Association, San Francisco, CA, January 5–7, 1996 (May 1996), 358–362.

24. There is a voluminous literature, but see especially Laurence J. Kotlikoff, "Privatizing Social Security at Home and Abroad," *American Economic Review* 86, no. 2, Papers and Proceedings of the Hundred and Eighth Annual Meeting of the American Economic Association, San Francisco, CA, January 5–7, 1996 (May 1996), 368–372; Laurence J. Kotlikoff, Kent A. Smetters, and Jan Walliser, "Social Security: Privatization and Progressivity," *American Economic Review* 88, no. 2, Papers and Proceedings of the Hundred and Tenth Annual Meeting of the American Economic Association (May 1998), 137–141; Steven F. Venti and David A. Wise, "The Cause of Wealth Dispersion at Retirement: Choice or Chance?" *American Economic Review* 88, no. 2, Papers and Proceedings of the Hundred and Tenth Annual Meeting of the American Economic Association (May 1998), 185–191, which argues that even high-income households do not adequately save for retirement; Peter A. Diamond, Alan J. Auerbach, and William G. Gale, "Macroeconomic Aspects of Social Security Reform," *Brookings Papers on Economic Activity*, vol. 1997, no. 2, 1997, 1–87. It is nonetheless difficult to find a contribution that estimates Social Security's positive contribution to the return of private assets through income stabilization.

25. As Keynes himself observes: "Moreover, even if over-investment in this sense was a normal characteristic of the boom, the remedy would not lie in clapping on a high rate of interest which would probably deter some useful investments, and might further diminish the propensity to consume, but in taking drastic steps, by redistributing income or otherwise, to stimulate the propensity to consume" (*General Theory* 1964, 320). This sentence by itself attacks decades of monetarist manipulation of the interest rate.

26. Jon E. Hilsenrath and Rebecca Buckman, "Factory Employment Is Falling Worldwide," *Wall Street Journal*, October 20, 2003.

27. Given the Republican Party's predisposition to ignore the needs of the poor, its recent passage of an expensive drug coverage plan for Medicare seems out of character. In fact, it is in character. First, the drug plan is a huge boon to the pharmaceutical companies that have been mainstay contributors to the party, ranking on a par with the tobacco companies. Second, the drug plan is a cynically efficient way to redistribute income to the social segment that actually votes, ignoring the vastly greater general need for medical coverage. It also targets the large population of retirees in Florida, about which no more need be said.

28. I disagree with the thesis that the Marxian and Keynesian analyses are compatible, but this is not the place to engage that debate. Marx depends too heavily on the immiseration thesis, a view of wages clearly derived from the classical economists. Max Weber heavily exploits Marx's dependency on this thesis in his attack on Marx's historiography in *Agrarian Sociology*. For a discussion, see Claudio Sardoni, "Keynes and Marx," in *A "Second Edition" of the General Theory*, eds. G.C. Harcourt and R.C. Riach, 2: 261–283 (New York: Routledge, 1997).

1

Keynes

An Activist's Life

J.M. Keynes was the most significant theorist of twentieth century economics, and his ideas continue to be the basis for influential developments in the field: in government and in academe, income, employment, health, trade, finance, and environmental policies have all been touched by Keynesian theory. Keynes also played key roles in major international economic policy events of the twentieth century, including World War I, the Great Depression, and World War II. This book focuses on the development of Keynes's economic ideas, their immediate predecessors, and their development after Keynes's death. The varied and immensely influential contributions that became "Keynesian economics" were linked to his personal life, his professional development, and his political commitments. This chapter briefly surveys these different sides of Keynes as a foundation for understanding his economic theory.

The primary reference tool for Keynes's writings is the *Collected Writings of John Maynard Keynes*, published by Macmillan. This complete compilation of Keynes's writings includes his personal correspondence with friends and professional publications. Its twenty-nine volumes were published between 1971 and 1983. Citations of the *Collected Writings* are found throughout this book, abbreviated *CW* followed by the volume and page number. Citations to volume 7 of the *Collected Writings* are to the *General Theory*, but readers in Commonwealth Countries may refer to any of the Macmillan editions of the last five decades, and readers in the United States to any of the Harcourt Brace Jovanovich editions. The pagination in all three sources is the same.

Keynes's Childhood, His Studies, His Clubs

John Maynard Keynes was born on June 6, 1883, in Cambridge, England. His family and social environment were highly conducive to his education and intellectual development. His mother, Florence Ada Keynes, was "modern" for the time. She was one of the first women students at Cambridge, and she later became actively engaged in politics, winning election to Cambridge's Town Council. She was known for her progressive ideas and advocacy of feminist causes.

Keynes's father, John Neville Keynes, was also highly accomplished. A professor of political economy and logic at Cambridge, he taught Marshallian economics and was best known for a book on the discipline's methodology titled *The Scope and Method of Political Economy.*

The young Keynes therefore grew up in an extremely stimulating environment. His family lived and moved in sophisticated intellectual circles. Their ideas and beliefs were cutting edge. Very early in his life, Keynes forged friendships with a number of intellectuals and artists. From his childhood he retained a solid friendship with the Stephen sisters. The two women are better known as Vanessa Bell (1879–1961), a renowned painter whose works hang today in London's Tate Gallery, and Virginia Woolf (1882–1941), the celebrated novelist.

Keynes's first chosen field of study was not political economy. As a student at Eton and then, in 1902, at King's College in Cambridge, he studied mathematics. His other interests included philosophy and medieval poetry. In 1903, he became a member of a club entirely devoted to philosophy, the Apostles. This group was heavily influenced by a young professor at Trinity College, G.E. Moore, author of the *Principia Ethica.* The Apostles' creed emphasized the pursuit of truth through a mix of intellectual austerity, moral rigor, and precise language that often contrasted with members' personal hedonism. Mathematical logic was a veritable dogma, even though Moore's philosophy also emphasized the role of intuition. Through the Apostles' club, Keynes became friends with men who represented a wide range of philosophical thought and literary interests. His social circle included Lytton Strachey and Leonard Woolf, who would eventually form the Bloomsbury group (see below). This "mathematical-philosophical period" gave Keynes the chance to shine in the eyes of illustrious figures such as Bertrand Russell and Alfred North Whitehead, who were then preparing their *Principia Mathematica,* a work that revolutionized philosophy in the English-speaking world. In 1909, Keynes defended a thesis on the logic of probability, written under Whitehead's supervision. The defense of this thesis was Keynes's first major intellectual contest. He proposed new and unconventional ideas. This thesis was published much later, in 1921, after extensive rewriting, under the title *A Treatise on Probability*. The probability theorists of the time were a bit shocked by the young Keynes.

Nonconformism was also evident in Keynes's London life from 1910 to 1920, as a member of the Bloomsbury group. The Stephen sisters, now married, sponsored two clubs devoted to the arts, literature, and philosophy. Duncan Grant, a painter with whom Keynes shared an apartment in London, introduced him into these circles in 1909. In 1916, he even shared a residence with Vanessa Bell at 46 Gordon Square. The Bloomsbury group was scandalous. Known for its freedom of spirit, it shocked an England that was barely out of the Victorian era. The Bloomsbury group discussed everything, without taboo. Keynes kept company with people noted for their intellectual passions. He met the philosopher Wittgenstein (1889–1951), who was staying at that time in Great Britain.

World War I, however, put our economist at odds with the pacifists of the Bloomsbury group. Keynes served as an economic advisor to the Treasury. The Bloomsbury group considered Keynes's participation in the war effort incompatible with their own views. In the 1920s, Keynes distanced himself from the group. In 1925, he married Lydia Lopokova, a classical ballerina who was not well received by the close-knit Bloomsbury group. Though he now was less involved in the literary scene, his interest in the arts did not weaken. Throughout his life, he sponsored a wide array of artistic shows and works; for example, in 1936, he helped found the Cambridge Arts Theater.

Keynes's Professional Life

Keynes's life was not limited to pure aesthetic consumption. His professional life overflowed with activity. In 1905, he seemed focused on a government career, seriously studying political economy as part of the entrance examination for the civil service. He studied with Alfred Marshall and Arthur C. Pigou. In 1906, he received a position at the India Office. His time in the India Office (1906–1908) was marked by profound boredom. Keynes later would say that his greatest deed at the India Office was to export a pureblood bull to Bombay. He nonetheless acquired sufficient knowledge of India's economy to publish, in 1913, *Indian Currency and Finance*. In it, he argued against basing the Indian currency on the gold standard and proposed, to the chagrin of "the city" (Britain's center of banking and finance), an independent central bank for India. Following his controversial probability thesis by four years, this proposal marked Keynes's second major intellectual engagement.

Having lost his taste for life as a public servant, Keynes returned to Cambridge in 1909. His thesis and Marshall's support won him a teaching position at King's College. For the rest of his life he remained affiliated with the university community.

Yet he also was kept a distance from academe: starting in 1920, he no longer received a regular salary for his teaching activity. He would spend Fridays and weekends at Cambridge and the rest of the week in London. He contributed regularly to the major economic journals and reviews. His courses and other works earned him respect at the university, as testified by a number of opportunities that came his way. He became editor of the *Economic Journal* in 1911, and, in 1913, secretary of the Royal Economic Society. The latter position allowed him to host a number of foreign visitors at Cambridge, some of whom came to stay, such as the economist Piero Sraffa. Keynes sponsored a political economy club on campus and participated in the great theoretical debates of the 1920s and 1930s, involving major economists such as Friedrich Hayek, Bertil Ohlin, and Jacques Rueff.

Keynes did not limit himself to academic pursuits. He was not only a theoretician, but also a pragmatic speculator in financial markets. He earned the wherewithal to pay for his multiple interests. Unlike most academic economists, many of whom have tried to do the same thing, he earned a fortune of £500,000 on the stock market. As bursar of King's College and secretary of the Royal Economic Society, he also enriched the endowments of the institutions he dearly loved. His success as a financial adviser, and also as a founder and director of several investment companies, earned him recognition in British banking and finance circles. He helped direct the investments of a number of insurance companies, including the National Mutual Life Insurance Company and the Provincial Insurance Company. From the 1920s till his death in 1946, Keynes had total financial independence, which proved a useful resource in his public battles against official positions.

Government Posts and Feckless Negotiations

Keynes's efforts in the 1920s to enhance his personal independence are explained by a stormy relationship with the government that was evident right at the beginning of his career. Aside from his short stint at the India Office, Keynes had official government jobs only during the two world wars. He joined the Treasury in 1915. In 1918 and 1919 he took part in the Versailles peace negotiations that brought World War I to a rather poor conclusion. In 1940, he was again a member of the Treasury staff, as an adviser who remained apart from the official internal hierarchy. He led the British delegation at the Bretton Woods conference (1943–1944), which established the new international monetary order that emerged in the aftermath of World War II. His disputes over the proper terms for concluding peace in 1919 and for establishing a new monetary system in 1945 were major public controversies, and he lost both times.

Keynes saw the punitive measures of the Treaty of Versailles as a scandal, and his protest against the treaty put him in the public spotlight. His intellectual independence was fully evident as he took on the job of championing a better peace. He had been assigned the job of calculating German reparations, using two criteria. The first was an appropriate indemnity for damages the Allies suffered during the war. The second was Germany's transfer capacity: the country's ability to earn a surplus of currencies necessary to make reparations payments. Keynes arrived at a moderate figure of £2 billion. The Bank of England disagreed, emphasizing reparations for damages rather than Germany's ability to pay, and advanced the figure of £24 billion. This was twelve times more than Germany's gross domestic product at the time. The Treaty of Versailles, as signed in June 1919, did not stipulate a definite amount to be paid. Instead, it created a reparations committee, which later fixed the amount due at £6.6 billion. The unyielding demands of the conquerors, who apparently wanted to crush Germany with a heavy reparations burden, convinced Keynes that his analysis would not be taken into consideration. On June 7, 1919, Keynes resigned from the Treasury and published *The Economic Consequences of the Peace,* one of the great polemical works in British history. Foreseeing that reparations would not be paid, Keynes somberly predicted new wars and revolutions in Europe. The book, written in only a few weeks with the aim of taking the policy debate to the public, enjoyed an immediate, worldwide impact. It earned Keynes a reputation as an ardent polemicist and visionary. History would vindicate his arguments.

Keynes's second spell at the Treasury, during World War II, did not bring him much more success in convincing the people in power. Although Keynes dominated the British delegation at the Bretton Woods conference, he was not, this time, up against his own government. His opponent was Harry Dexter, who had been director of monetary research and was then assistant secretary of the U.S. Treasury. The American "White Plan," in its final form, reflected the conservatism of the American Congress and sought to establish the new international monetary system on the basis of the gold standard.

Keynes opposed the gold standard as a "barbarous relic," as he had derisively referred to gold in 1923. His plan called for breaking with the gold standard and proposed instead an international monetary unit of account, the bancor, that would be issued by an international central bank. The International Clearing Union's bankers' currency would circulate among nations and substitute for gold as a unit of account. Keynes's proposal had two objectives: to erase the asymmetry in the distribution of gold among nations and, even more important, to create overdraft accounts, or emergency credit, that would help countries maintain the stability of their currencies over long periods of time. The idea was to eliminate a situation where trade deficits or surpluses led almost immediately to currency fluctuations.

Keynes's vigorous, well-thought-out arguments earned him the respect of the American delegation, but failed to convince its members. Even so, Keynes's experience in the Treasury this time around was not entirely negative. As a key adviser to the Treasury, he helped organize the British war economy. He helped develop principles of national accounting that were influential in other countries. The Depression economies of the 1930s had motivated Keynes's investigation of unemployment in the *General Theory*. The key features of the Depression were stagnant or falling demand, high unemployment, low investment, falling wages, and falling prices. In *How to Pay for the War* (1940, *CW* 9:367–439), written during his Treasury years, Keynes developed tools for analyzing, within the framework of his *General Theory*, the problem of an "overheated economy." The symptoms of an overheated economy were exactly the reverse of the Depression: high war-induced demand for weapons and goods of all sorts, high levels of employment, increasing investment, rising wages, and rising prices.

Keynes's Political Engagements: The Manifestos, the Pamphlets, and the Economic History of the 1920s and 1930s

This brief biographical account would not be complete without mentioning Keynes's longest-running policy engagement: his battle against the

Conservative Party and its anachronistic economic views. Keynes thought that the entrenched orthodoxy of the Conservatives, especially when it came to gold and the return to prewar parity, was responsible for Britain's deep, long-lasting economic crisis of the 1920s. The Conservatives sought to restore the value of the British pound, relative to gold, to its level of 1914, before the inflation of World War I. In his battle against this orthodoxy, Keynes resorted to what we might call short-range but effective weapons: short essays and pamphlets. He also developed what we might call, by analogy, long-range intercontinental missiles: his major theoretical works. A discussion of these works will occupy several of the following chapters. Here, we will mention them briefly, as well as his shorter works.

In addition to his academic output, Keynes had a knack for powerfully argued, rapid-fire responses to the economic, social, and political issues of his day. The most celebrated was his *Economic Consequences of the Peace* (1919), discussed above. However, foreign policy was not his only concern, and his essays on domestic policy issues show the same technique: rapid-fire responses, followed often by the political equivalent of hand-to-hand combat. He praised some policies and heaped scorn on others. Keynes's short articles and pamphlets were designed to influence public opinion and government officials, not economic theorists. Two of his well-known works of this kind are *The Economic Consequences of Mr. Churchill* (1925) and *Can Lloyd George Do It?* (1929). Many of these essays were collected and edited by Keynes under the title of *Essays in Persuasion* (1931). This book included a number of his articles that had appeared in *The Nation and Athenaeum*, an influential publication in which Keynes's articles enjoyed the company of contributions from other well-known political and literary names. These included socialists such as H.N. Brailsford and G.D.H. Cole; the political scientist Harold Laski; writers such David Garnett and Leonard Woolf; and J.A. Hobson, the maverick economic theorist of underconsumption. The periodical was at the time controlled by the Liberal Party, with which Keynes often sided in his public policy debates.

Keynes's message can be stated in a few words. The principal economic policies adopted by the Conservatives and implemented by Mr. Churchill starting in 1924 were wrong. The strategy of returning the pound to its prewar parity with gold had put a brake on Britain's economic dynamism. British products were losing market share abroad because of the overvaluation of the British pound, which also led to a trade deficit. Moreover, the burden of artificially maintaining the old parity level of the pound was causing the Bank of England to set its discount rate (the rate at which it made money available to other banks, influencing other commercial rates) at an onerously high level. The high interest rate thwarted private investment and slowed down the economy. In Great Britain, high levels of unemployment appeared very early, much sooner than in the United States, France, and other countries where unemployment followed on the heels of the financial crisis of 1929. As early as 1928, Britain already had a million unemployed workers.

The policy recommended by the Conservatives to solve the crisis struck Keynes as wrong-headed. Rather than leave the pound alone, they sought to improve Great Britain's international competitiveness by following a policy of austerity—monetary and budgetary discipline that they hoped would, with time, lead to lower prices and wages. In theory, automatic stabilizers (the exchange rate adjustment mechanism) advocated by David Ricardo (1772–1828) should lead to a lowering of prices, or deflation. According to the classical economists, in a fixed exchange rate system based on gold, a commercial trade deficit causes gold to leave the country. This in turn decreases the currency in circulation and finally, according to the quantity theory of money, leads to lowered prices. Lower prices make goods more attractive to foreign buyers and therefore revive a country's foreign trade.

In other words, the effects of trade deficits and trade surpluses are corrected automatically by changes in the general level of prices for goods and wages for workers. Keynes argued against this position: "On grounds of social justice no case can be made out for reducing the wages of the miners. They are the victims of the economic juggernaut. They represent in the flesh the 'fundamental adjustments' engineered by the Treasury and the Bank of England to satisfy the impatience of the City fathers to bridge the 'moderate gap' between $4.40 and $4.86 [the exchange rate between the pound sterling and the dollar]" (CW 9:223).

Keynes thus supported a policy opposite to that of the Conservative Party. In 1929, he persuaded Lloyd George, then leader of the Liberal Party, to adopt a public works program. Since the exchange rate adjustment mechanism, an outdated concept of the nineteenth century, was not working, Keynes argued that the state should assume responsibility for making the economy work again. The Liberals were politically very weak and would never again win a British election. But Keynes was given a chance to defend his ideas on two different commissions, one convened by the Conservatives, the other by the Laborites. Formed to find solutions to the economic crisis, these were the Macmillan Commission and the Economic Advisory Council.

As the above quotation shows, however, Keynes's arguments had both moral and social dimensions. For reasons of social justice, deflation was not acceptable. Keynes felt, however, a need to support his arguments against economic orthodoxy, and his support for public works, with a strictly economic line of argument. Deflation cannot in any way be a cause of economic efficiency. This is the object of his theoretical work: Keynes's political tracts are therefore linked to his formal economics.

His formal economic theory, concisely stated, consists of what Patinkin (1976, 7) has called a "monetary trilogy." In 1923, Keynes published *A Tract on Monetary Reform* (*CW* 4), the first part of this trilogy. Here Keynes argued against a fixed gold parity for the pound, saying it should float. He thus preferred external instability, in the value of the pound against other currencies, over internal instability, in the level of prices and wages. In other words, he was attacking the principle of automatic stabilizers. In 1930, the second part of the "monetary trilogy" appeared as *A Treatise on Money* (*CW* 5, 6). In 1936, the third part of the "monetary trilogy," *The General Theory of Employment, Interest, and Money* (*CW* 7), was published. The *Treatise* and the *General Theory* will be looked at in greater detail in later chapters.

Taken together, the three works were a rising crescendo against economic orthodoxy. The *Tract* of 1923 made, relative to what came later, relatively modest arguments against orthodox notions of monetary laws and international trade. The later *Treatise* and, much more fundamentally, the *General Theory* advanced arguments that were more than just different; they were revolutionary. In the opinion of Keynes's more radical interpreters, they attacked orthodoxy at its roots.

In this respect, Patinkin's characterization of these works as a monetary trilogy suggests that they are more homogeneous than in fact they are. There is such a huge break between the first two books and the last that the word "trilogy" seems applicable mainly because of the three works' common focus on money. For this is, in fact, the axis of Keynes's attack on classical economic theory.

Conclusion

Keynes died on April 21, 1946. What were the most outstanding aspects of his brilliantly diverse life? It is clear that Keynes was not just another university professor. Unlike most of the great twentieth-century names of economic science, Keynes did not earn his bread from engaging in teaching and learned academic disputes with his colleagues. He was perfectly at home in business and political circles. Sometimes he was even directly responsible for government decisions. This was true not only in Great Britain but also abroad: he participated in drafting major international treaties and even met with President Franklin Roosevelt some months before enactment of the first New Deal programs in the United States.

Keynes's work is therefore part of economics's role in history, as well as part of the history of economic thought. That is its strength and weakness. A political adviser must act with great speed on questions of the moment. This commitment sometimes works against the insulated, thorough approach to theoretical questions that the pure academic prefers. In other words, Keynes's passionate commitment to seeing Great Britain consign its false gods (the gold standard and laissez-faire) to the flames made his work that of an activist as well as a theorist. Though being an activist may seem to load Keynes's work with connotations that weaken his claim to being a theoretician, it is in fact his *activism* that supplies a key to reading and understanding his work.

Nonetheless, the next chapter focuses on the history of ideas, leaving aside Keynes's political activism. Our task in the next chapter is to show the state of economic theory at precisely the moment in history when it was about to undergo what we now call the Keynesian revolution. As we shall see, the work of many major figures had prepared the way for Keynes's breakthroughs.

2

Economic Thought on the Eve of the *General Theory*

However broad his career experience, Keynes was ever the professional economist. His research articles and private correspondence engaged his contemporaries within the context of the economic theory of his time. To understand Keynes's work, therefore, we must review the intellectual context in which it developed. The English tradition of *partial equilibrium*, represented by Marshall and Pigou, and the theory of *general equilibrium*, advanced by Walras and Fisher, are presented below. This detour into the history of economic thought will clarify Keynes's core concepts.

The English Tradition of Partial Equilibrium Theory

Keynes was first and foremost influenced by his teachers, Alfred Marshall (1842–1924) and Arthur Cecil Pigou (1877–1959), the two most well-known British economists at the beginning of the twentieth century.

Alfred Marshall and Sectors of Economic Activity

In Britain at the beginning of the twentieth century, Alfred Marshall was considered the "pope" of economics; it was his mission, in his own words, to build economics's "cathedral." His *Principles of Economics* (1890) was the basis of economics teaching in university courses. As Keynes said, "We are all students of Marshall."

The Role of Time in Marshall's Principles

One of Marshall's goals was to show the compatibility of classical economic theory (as developed by Adam Smith and David Ricardo between 1776 and 1823) and neoclassical theory (also called marginalist theory, dating from 1870). Time, and the sector dynamics described by Marshall, constitutes the necessary elements for synthesizing the two bodies of work. This Marshallian synthesis explains why Keynes could lump into the same term, "classical," the whole body of orthodox economic theory. More important, a review of Marshall's synthesis gives us insight into the most crucial and lively questions of economic theory during Keynes's lifetime.

Toward the end of the 1870s, there were two conflicting theories of the determination of the relative value of a good. The classical group, developing Ricardo's insights, argued that the exchange relationship of goods (their price) was regulated by their costs of production. The marginalist group countered that the exchange relationship of goods is determined by the relative utility of the last unit consumed. Do *production and supply* considerations determine the market's equilibrium price, or do *demand and utility* determine it? Marshall's response is clear: the two pairs of influences are like the twin blades of a scissors. However, depending on what moment we observe, and depending on what blade of the scissors is in motion, we will give more importance to one or the other of the two relationships. Time is therefore an essential component of economic analysis. Marshall identifies three periods: the very short term (or market period), the short term, and the long term. In a celebrated passage, Marshall advances this thesis in the parable of the fish market. Figures 2.1, 2.2, and 2.3 illustrate Marshall's reasoning.

The very short period. The very short period (Figure 2.1) is the moment of the actual market transaction. It is defined as the moment when the fishing fleet returns to port and unloads its fish. Market supply is perfectly rigid: in the market, in this case the fishing pier, a vertical line represents supply. Price depends entirely on the level of demand. For example, a sudden news announcement about mad cow disease drives consumers to prefer fish to beef. This demand shock would produce a rise in prices. At the level of the firms (each fishing boat), a windfall profit would be realized. The choice of the quantity Q^*_i (at the minimum of the average cost) as the firm's assumed initial offered supply will be justified at the end of our parable.

50

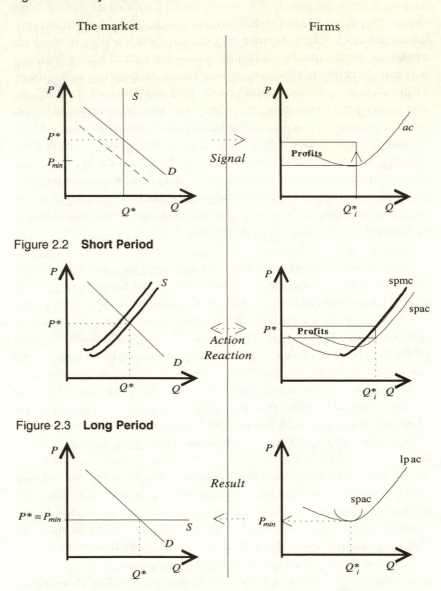

Figure 2.1 **Very Short Period**

The market

Firms

Signal

Figure 2.2 **Short Period**

< · · · >

Action

Reaction

Figure 2.3 **Long Period**

Result

Q = quantity; Q^* = equilibrium quantity; P = price; P^* = equilibrium price; ac = average cost; spac = short period average cost; spmc = short period marginal cost; lpac = long period average cost; P_{min} = price corresponding to the average cost curve; Q_i is the quantity supplied by firm i; Q^*_i is the quantity at equilibrium; S = supply; D = demand.

The short period. The short period (Figure 2.2) may range from several days to several months. It is more rigorously defined as the lag time required for firms to react to the demand shock, but without modifying the capital stock. The fishermen may extend their workday or work on weekends, but the number of fishing boats—the capital stock—remains the same. Reacting to the upswing in demand, each fishing boat pushes its production to the maximum profit: the point at which its marginal cost equals the market price. Each ship will hire more employees and spend more time at sea. Each ship's additional offer of fish for sale increases the total supply of fish in the market. Intersecting with the total demand, this supply determines the price. However, during this time, the continued existence of windfall profits entices new entrants into this sector of economic activity. The new firms extend the total fleet of ships, and the total supply of fish in the market increases in successive stages as depicted in the left panel of the graph.

The long period. The long period (Figure 2.3) takes our parable to its conclusion. During the long period, the total capital and the number of firms adjust to accommodate demand. First, each business has had the opportunity to reduce its costs; the "long period average cost" (lpac) curve encompasses the "short period average cost" (spac) curve, which means that each fishing boat has had a chance to optimize its production techniques for the new conditions in the fishing industry. Second, at the level of the total activity of the fishing sector of the economy, the windfall profit signal has triggered an adjustment in the number of firms. The size of the fishing fleet has increased, meaning new capital has entered production and new competitive firms have been created. In the market, total supply increases, which pushes down the equilibrium price. This process continues until the windfall profit has been eliminated. In the long term, therefore, the entry of new capital causes the new, higher level of demand to be satisfied at the competitive price determined by the minimum average cost of the firms. (We assume identical costs. If we assume differing costs among firms, the most efficient firms will earn higher profits, also called economic rents).

Marshall's description of the investment dynamics of a single sector (the word "sector" today is usually preferred to his word, "branch") illustrates a number of points relevant to the study of Keynes. First, this description explains Keynes's position regarding the existence of a single classical paradigm in economics. Marshall's use of time permits a logical synthesis between classical and neoclassical considerations: in the short period, consumer preferences determine prices; in the long period, the costs of production determine them. The marginalists solve the short-period problem, and David Ricardo solves the long-term problem.

With everyone in apparent agreement, the debate seemed closed. In any case, Keynes never returned to the question of value. More fundamentally, the Marshallian dynamic is a superb demonstration (though under restrictive assumptions, as we shall see) of how free enterprise allocates resources in society. In the parable of the fish market, demand and supply work to adjust the productive structure of an economy to consumers' needs. In the first phase, when supply is inelastic, the new preference for fish is rationed by price. As time passes, increased demand attracts additional resources into the fishing industry. Excess or windfall profits play a transitory but crucial role: providing the mechanism by which an adjustment in investment is made. Marshall's description of the market almost becomes a panegyric. And we may say that on this point Keynes let himself be convinced.

Marshall's Theoretical Dead Ends: The Very Long Period, the Question of Returns to Scale, and Sraffa's Critique

The principal interest for us in studying Marshallian market adjustments lies in their limitations. The first objection usually raised against Marshall resides in his partial equilibrium approach. Marshall deliberately neglects the question of the fish market's interaction with other markets. Precisely *what* is going on in the meat market during this wonderful adjustment process? Might there not be interactive effects between the two markets, which could call into question the fish market's ability to reach a long-period equilibrium in the manner previously described?

Lacking the tools to answer this question, Marshall set it aside. The economic science of his time, in spite of repeated attempts, had not been able to pose, or answer, the question adequately. We will return to this problem farther on, in a section devoted to Walras's development of general equilibrium theory.

Marshall himself suggested a second objection to the partial equilibrium approach that questioned the evolution of the stationary state established in the long period. In fact, this objection opens the debate on economic dynamics to a new temporal context: the very long period. The difficulty is this: At the end of the long period, we enter a Ricardian world where there is no economic progress because the economy is pos-tulated to be in a stationary state. After adjustments between demand and supply have been made, the economy is stuck: the prices of goods offered in one sector are strictly determined at the minimum of the aver-age cost, with no further possibility for development. Decreasing re-turns in the various sectors of the economy (identical to the assumption of average costs in the form of a U) end up creating a stationary state where prices can neither rise, because of competition, nor fall, because of costs. The economy appears to be inert, with no potential for growth. Marshall was very unhappy with this conclusion, which missed obvi-ous, empirical truths of economic reality: productivity increases in dif-ferent sectors, their effects on the entire economic structure, and, of course, the existence of a positive overall growth rate in the major capi-talist economies. (Unlike Ricardo, Marshall had the tremendous pro-ductivity gains of the late nineteenth-century industrial revolution to contend with.)

To resolve the conflict between theory and reality, Marshall offered the possibility of "external effects" between firms in the same sector. He sought to explain how firms in the same sector, in the very long period, manage to supply their product under conditions of decreasing costs (or increasing returns to scale). A given sector, like the fishing industry, could be graphed as shown in Figure 2.4.

Marshall had to pass, as he himself put it, from a "mechanical anal-ogy" to a "biological analogy." The firms of a given sector were not passive objects under the exclusive influence of competition, but gained from one another in the same way as the parts of a living body. Marshall seems therefore to have settled on a view that the overall returns on a sector of production would grow. And that is finally how he chose to explain economic progress.

But the story does not end there. In 1926, Piero Sraffa, a friend of Keynes, came to Cambridge for a short stay that became rather long (he died there in 1983). His 1926 article was of tremendous importance for the future of economics: "The Laws of Return under Competitive Con-ditions." Sraffa, arguing against Marshall's analysis, observed the logi-cal incompatibility of increasing economic returns from individual sectors *and*, simultaneously, competition between firms. One could not have it both ways. Either the returns to scale were in fact increasing in indi-vidual sectors, meaning the biggest firm would produce at the least cost and establish a monopoly in that sector; or, competition could be as-

Figure 2.4 **Very Long Period**

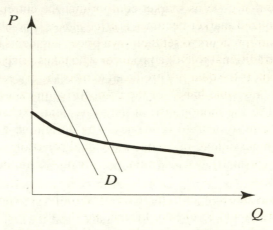

sumed to continue to exist, but in this case, it would be impossible to sustain the hypothesis of increasing returns to scale.

This logical criticism of Marshallian dynamics, though it has been resolved since through a systematic use of externalities, caused a commotion in the world of economics. Two related dogmas, one positing decreasing returns over time and the other positing that competition exerts a downward pressure on prices, had been considered essential to economic reasoning and partial equilibrium analysis. Now they were recognized as mutually contradictory. Moreover, this criticism suggested two parallel research agendas for economists least attached to traditional dogma. One agenda was to abandon the partial equilibrium perspective and see how increasing returns, or constant returns, might be integrated into an *interactive* conception of markets. That was the path that Sraffa himself would follow and that modern economic theory has revisited with its theories of endogenous growth. On the other hand, one could abandon the assumption of competition, and analyze monopolistic markets or conditions of imperfect competition. This last path, first put forward by Joan Robinson (1933) and Edward Chamberlin (1933), proved to be, at least at that time, the most attractive.

The theory of imperfect competition led its originators to novel conclusions. Economic decisions, always considered rational and profit maximizing, are placed within a new context. Firms' activities are determined by such factors as their market positions (dominant or minor market shares, and their ability to capture specific buyers) and the information available to themselves and their customers. Viewed this way, one type of decision maker stands out as essential to establishing the dynamic that governs market equilibrium: the entrepreneur, who in a monopolized market becomes a *price maker.* The ability of monopolistic entrepreneurs to set their own prices augments their powers beyond the traditional role of a producer who takes price as set by the market and alters the quantity produced to meet the price. The famous, impersonal, "invisible hand" of the competitive market becomes the visible hand of the monopolist: at the same time, exchange markets lose their claim to "Pareto efficiency" (by definition, a situation in which it is impossible to make one individual better off without making another worse off), because monopolistic profits diminish the well-being of others.

Keynes was no stranger to these debates, for he corresponded regularly with Sraffa and Robinson. Indeed, we shall see that his analyses were integrated into these theoretical developments, which tended to deemphasize the role of market mechanisms in regulating production. This led Keynes to emphasize the behavior of entrepreneurs, who enjoyed a dominant, or asymmetric, position in the market. After his death, his principle of effective demand, for example, would be explicitly linked (by, for example, J.P. Benassy 1984, 1993, 1995) to an analysis of imperfect competition.

Arthur Cecil Pigou: The Real Balance Effect

If one wanted to characterize the spiritual children of Marshall, Keynes would be the youngest child, rebellious and ungrateful; Pigou would be the oldest, well behaved and obedient to his father. In Keynes's writings, the contrast between their personalities is pushed to excess: Pigou is turned into a reverent symbol of classical economics. He becomes the leader of orthodoxy whose sophisms and conformism must be repudiated. Pigou, for his part, willingly played the role Keynes set out for him.

Marshall and Pigou's Monetary Theory: Macroeconomics and the Real Balance Effect

After the publication of his *Principles,* Marshall believed that the most important work in his field had been done. The great questions had been asked, and their answers given or outlined. Most especially, aggregate economic activity could logically be explained by the microeconomic behaviors already discussed above (the dynamics of economic sectors). There remained one question to resolve: that of money and its integration into the general equilibrium. Money, moreover, was the point of entry chosen by the Cambridge economists to develop macroeconomics. Indeed, to this day, the notion of *monetary economics* is used as a synonym of *macroeconomics*, especially in Britain and North America. The major international economics journals still aggregate *monetary economics* and *macroeconomics* in their index classifications.

Shortly before he died, Marshall published *Money, Credit and Commerce* (1923), which dealt with money and its macroeconomic effects. Pigou developed these ideas further. Among the classical economists, money was a veil: variations in the quantity of money had no effect on the level or structure of real economic activity. Changes in the money supply influence only the general level of prices. This is the real activity-monetary dichotomy. The usual approach to this dichotomy is through Fisher's equation, which allows us to calculate the inflationary consequences of the quantity of money put into circulation. The Cambridge economists adopted a parallel approach. Rather than develop a theory of monetary *movement*, as Fisher did in asking how and why money circulates, the English economists asked, why does money stay *at rest*, and why and how is it kept out of circulation? This focus pushed them to the theory of real money balances.

Marshall and Pigou studied the reasons that cause economic agents to hang on to their money. They noted that as an instrument of exchange, money is held to permit future exchanges. Economic agents accumulate cash balances with future transactions in mind. More precisely, the theory of real money balances holds that economic agents try to hang on to enough money to provide a constant purchasing power. The nominal value of the demand for money is therefore exactly proportional to the sum of transactions. This hypothesis takes the following form,

$$M^d = k \, p \, T,$$

where M^d = the demand for money; p = the general price level; T = the volume of transactions; and k = a factor indicating the proportion between desired money balances and the total of all transactions.

This expression is simply a definition of k, the proportion between money balances and transactions that agents want to maintain in the

Figure 2.5   **Pigou's Story of the Real Balance Effect**

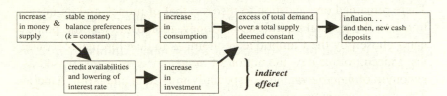

aggregate. Nonetheless, the theory of real balances is used by Pigou to argue for a *quantitative* relationship between the quantity of money in circulation and the price level. His causal reasoning is schematized in Figure 2.5. The illustration shows the consequences of a *monetary expansion*, that is, new money created by political authorities. In the first phase, the increase in the money supply meets a *stable, predetermined desire to hold money balances.* This desire is shown as a fixed ratio, k. The new money therefore exceeds the demand for money; its holders do not want to keep it, so they look for a way to spend it. Here two pathways are possible, corresponding to the direct and indirect effects of the Cambridge equation advanced by Pigou and Marshall. Either the excess money is spent on goods or it is placed in financial markets, where it tends to push the interest rate down.

Whichever path is taken, the total level of demand rises due to increases in one or both of its C^d (consumption) and I^d (investment). Here, Pigou, supposing that the *total supply of goods has been fixed in advance,* sees an inevitable increase in prices as an adjustment to the monetarily inspired increase in demand. More succinctly, inflation follows a monetary expansion. However, as a result, cash balances desired by economic agents are modified. As shown in the illustration, the increase in the nominal level of transactions (the general increase in the prices of all goods) leads economic agents to increase their cash balances, so that the purchasing power of the money they keep in reserve remains the same. The excess money supply has been absorbed.

Such is Pigou's position in his *Industrial Fluctuations* (1927). Pigou argues that in the long run, the excess supply of money is totally absorbed by the action of the real balance effect in inflationary conditions. The effect of a monetary expansion is therefore nil, except for increases in the price level. Economic agents have compensated, via the real balance effect, for the increases in the money supply. The linchpin of this argument lies in its hypothesis of a rigid, or fixed, level of supply of goods in the short term. Keynes will closely examine this argument, whether it is based on the Marshallian theory of short period supply, or whether it is based on the full use of factor inputs. In his *Treatise on Money* (1930), Keynes will criticize and finally endorse Pigou's argument. In his *General Theory* (1936), he will argue against it.

Pigou's Theory of Unemployment

Pigou did not stop with monetary analysis. In 1933, he published his *Theory of Unemployment*, his response to the depression that had plagued Britain since the mid-1920s. The Cambridge professor, following the precepts of the most orthodox classical theory, concluded that labor was underutilized in Britain because it cost too much. Union demands kept labor costs too high, which discouraged the hiring of workers. Moreover, this wage rigidity prevented a lowering of the general price level (deflation), which would have improved the country's international competitiveness and compensated for the overvalued British pound (see Chapter 1 of this book). Pigou's political-economic solution: reduce wages, so as to make hiring Britain's unemployed and exporting to foreign markets profitable.

This proposal was also supported by Pigou's real balance effect. According to Pigou, the deflation that must follow the reduction of wages would have to be accompanied by a reduction in cash holdings. Lower prices would increase the real value of cash, raising its purchasing power beyond the desired level. Not needing this extra consuming power in the form of savings, people would reduce their cash balances by spending. This fortuitous increase in spending would support the overall level of demand in the economy and counteract the depressive effect of wage reductions. It is easy to see that Pigou attributed to the real balance effect a new compensating power: the effects of increasing or decreasing real balances are added to the classic self-regulating mechanisms of markets and prices. Pigou's arguments reinforce the classical view and at the same time diminish the negative social consequences of price adjustments. Keynes would later oppose this *Pigou effect* (a synonym for real balance effect) with his own *wealth effect*. Contrary to Pigou, Keynes argues that deflation diminishes the net wealth of debtors (by increasing the real cost of their debt repayments), which forces them to limit their spending, causing the depression to worsen.

Keynes paid close attention to the ideas developed by Pigou. The relationships governing prices, economic activity, and money became central to Keynes's own work and, indeed, remain at the heart of macroeconomics. In particular, the reasons given by Keynes for the desire to hold money, though extremely innovative, would never have been possible without the preliminary work of Pigou on the real balance effect. Thus, one can say that Keynes was put on the trail of these ideas by his mentor. But, having explored the issues, he came to different conclusions. For his part, Pigou in the end conceded Keynes's arguments, acknowledging that massive short-term unemployment is possible and that the classical theory had not sufficiently taken this into account. (Pigou's concession to Keynes may be read in *Keynes's General Theory: A Retrospective View,* 1950.)

The General Equilibrium Perspective

In Britain, general equilibrium theory was not widely used among Keynes's predecessors and contemporaries. The pragmatic British preferred to explore the logical consequences of partial equilibrium, from which they derived important economic insights. However, the Cambridge economists were aware of the weaknesses inherent in their oft-used phrase "all other things being equal" (sometimes written in Latin, *ceteris paribus*), which they used to show that they were studying a single market in isolation from all the rest. John Hicks (1904–1989), heavily influenced by the work of Walras and an occasional correspondent with Keynes, helped to spread the general equilibrium approach in Great Britain.

Leon Walras and Interdependence

The inventor of the general equilibrium approach to economics was a Frenchman who was not well known in the academic circles of his own country. Leon Walras (1834–1910) developed ideas in 1874 that, emphasizing the interdependence of markets, superficially conflicted with Marshall's approach but ultimately reinforced many of his results. In the next few pages we will summarize Walras's views and look more broadly at the logic of general equilibrium. Formal presentations of general equilibrium can be found in many textbooks, so we will focus on certain intuitive aspects of this theory and also on the problem of how to integrate money. We shall highlight the positive aspects of general equilibrium as well as certain logical dead ends, especially as these provide insight into the development of Keynesian theory.

General Equilibrium Theory: Its Intrinsic Logic

General equilibrium theory begins with the interconnectedness of markets. *Prevailing conditions* of supply and demand in one market are not independent of *prevailing conditions* in other markets. We emphasize *prevailing conditions* because at any moment these markets could as easily be in disequilibrium (a condition of excess demand or of excess supply) as in equilibrium. We can explore the interdependence of markets in two ways. First, we can look at the *substitutability* and *complementarity* of goods. *Substitutable goods* can replace one another, perhaps imperfectly, in meeting the needs of market participants. The price of one good on the market interacts positively with the demand for the other good. For example, the prevailing conditions in the pineapple market depend on the banana market, because price movements in bananas might induce people to buy more or less pineapples. For *complementary goods*, a change in demand for one will cause demand for the other to change in the same direction. Prevailing conditions in the automobile market and the automotive tire market are thus linked.

The second way to look at the interdependence of markets is more theoretically profound, especially for the study of Keynes. This approach focuses on the *income constraints* that affect the behavior of market actors. Every person, and every household, has a certain amount of disposable income that results from the sale of certain goods (especially labor). This income is used to satisfy household needs, meaning it is used to buy either consumption goods or savings instruments. The interdependence of the two is clear: the *purchase* of goods is limited by the *household income* gained from the *sale* of still other goods. (Later we will call this the purchase-sale identity.) For example, in a given household, the purchase of consumption goods necessarily relies on two other conditions: first, it depends on the level of purchases made elsewhere (capital goods, savings instruments, and so on). Second, it depends on the total sale of another good, *labor*, which is by far the major source of household income. From this it becomes clear that the markets for goods, for capital, and for labor cannot be separated from one another: we need a *general* analysis of equilibrium.

Among the marginalists, Walras has the special merit of emphasizing the interdependence of markets. In his view, the study of equilibrium must explicitly integrate the various interactions among markets. This thesis is well known. For *n* different goods, there exist *n* different markets, where there are *n* demand and supply functions. Each function is determined by summing the behavior patterns of the different households, which depend on the different prices for goods (as determined by the interdependence of prevailing conditions in each market). The *excess demand* (*E,* the difference between supply, *S,* and demand, *D*) of *n* goods is written as follows:

$$E_1(p_1, \ldots, p_k, \ldots, p_n) = D_1(p_1, \ldots, p_k, \ldots, p_n) - S_1(p_1, \ldots, p_k, \ldots, p_n);$$

$$E_k(p_1, \ldots, p_k, \ldots, p_n) = D_k(p_1, \ldots, p_k, \ldots, p_n) - S_k(p_1, \ldots, p_k, \ldots, p_n);$$

$$E_n(p_1, \ldots, p_k, \ldots, p_n) = D_n(p_1, \ldots, p_k, \ldots, p_n) - S_n(p_1, \ldots, p_k, \ldots, p_n).$$

These *n* values describe the prevailing conditions of the different markets of an economic system. In certain markets, $(1, 2, \ldots, g)$, the excess demand levels are positive, meaning there is more demand than goods to satisfy it. In other markets $(g + 1, g + 2, \ldots, n)$ the excess demand levels are negative, meaning more goods are being offered for sale than there is demand to buy them. However, Walras, who always sought to be as clear and logical as possible, does not see these *prevailing conditions* as free from each other's influence. Recalling the purchase-sale identity that we have already outlined, he observed that any particular excess demand is the necessary result of all the others. For a given individual, one can always deduce, from his income constraints, his behavior on the *n*th market, so long as we know his behavior on all the other $(n-1)$ markets. The balance between the availability of goods and the uses for them, insofar as they are known in other markets, always allows one to deduce the unknown elements of the last market.

Mathematically summing all individuals' transactions in all markets, we can always deduce the balance of transactions in the *n*th market, if we know the transactions in the other $n-1$ markets. *The pre-vailing conditions in* n *– 1 markets determine the prevailing conditions in the* n*th market.* This principle is known as *Walras's law.* Following from the accounting identity between purchases and sales, it helps us assess the logical coherence of the entire approach. Walras' law allows us to drop one of the n excess demand functions from the study of economic equilibrium.

But what is equilibrium? The principle of equilibrium among economists refers to an accounting criterion in the desires of economic agents: the fact that once they have formulated their individual supply and demand of goods, none of the proposed transactions remains unsatisfied. A *Walrasian equilibrium* assumes, therefore, that each instance of demand is covered by an equivalent offer of supply.[1] The sum of the excess demands is zero:

$$E_1 (p_1, \ldots, p_k, \ldots, p_n) = 0;$$

$$E_k (p_1, \ldots, p_k, \ldots, p_n) = 0;$$

$$E_n (p_1, \ldots, p_k, \ldots, p_n) = 0.$$

The vector of the price in each economic sector $(p^*_1, p^*_2, \ldots, p^*_n)$, which leads to the zeroing out of all excess demands, corresponds strictly to the Walrasian equilibrium. Following Walras's law, we need employ only $n-1$ equations; the last is redundant.

This state of affairs could seriously mathematically hamper the theory of general equilibrium, because, everything considered, we have only $n-1$ equations to determine n unknowns. To resolve this problem, we can imagine, with Walras, that one of the goods becomes the unit of value of all the others. We can measure the price of the exchange of goods in one of the total number n of goods: for example, sheep. In a world where all prices are set in sheep units, a cow is worth two sheep, a rooster is worth 0.2 sheep, and so on. One of the goods is thus transformed into a *standard of value,* or, since Walras's French is still used, a *numéraire.* The price of the *numéraire* is by definition 1 (one sheep is worth one sheep). With one value known, there remain only $n-1$ exchange relationships to determine with $n-1$ independent equations. This makes a solution determinate.

Such are Walras's theoretical innovations on general equilibrium. The equilibrium is logically defined by a price vector, or movement of prices, which insures a clearing of markets—everything offered for sale is in fact sold. Two points must be made here, because they are relevant to what follows concerning the integration of money into this analysis. Walras's *Elements of Pure Economics, or the Theory of Social Wealth* (1874) takes very small steps. He limits himself first to an *exchange economy* (his simplifying assumptions are that goods are not produced, and are bartered, not exchanged for money). He then considers a *production economy* and finally moves to a *production economy with money*. Walras clearly wants to save for last the delicate problem of money (which is linked to, but distinct from, the problem of the *numéraire*). We will come back to this problem. In any case, as to the choice of *numéraire,* Walras considers it unimportant insofar as economic agents are considered rational. That is, they respond not to the level of prices but to relative prices, the ratio at which goods exchange for one another. The use of roosters, rather than sheep, as a *numéraire* would, in the example above, multiply nominal price levels by five. But economic agents, recognizing this purely nominal shift for what it is, will not modify their behavior.

We will return to this supposed lack of sensitivity to nominal price levels in Walrasian models, because it is at the heart of a dichotomy between real and monetary effects that Keynes will challenge.

General Equilibrium: A Host of Problems

Walras's general equilibrium approach is as interesting because of its limitations as because of its merits. Three categories of problems emerge: problems of pure mathematics; problems of price convergence and the supposed coordination of an auctioneer; and problems of pure economics.

Problems of pure mathematics. The mathematical problems are of two orders. First, we must consider the *existence of an equilibrium.* Walras postulates the existence of equilibrium based on the simple concordance of the number of equations with the number of unknown variables. However, it is well known that such a postulate is insufficient. Nonetheless, Walras gets some credit for having anticipated the solution that was discovered after his death. Using standard assumptions, such as the existence of rational agents, Arrow and Debreu (1954) demonstrated that an equilibrium set of prices does exist. But that did not solve the second problem, which is whether there is a *unique* equilibrium. That has not been established; far from it. The Walrasian equations might permit any number of solutions, corresponding to different levels of transactions in *n* markets. Economic analysis has labored long on this question. In 1933, the German mathematician Abraham Wald demonstrated the existence of a unique equilibrium under the restrictive assumption of gross ("over-all") substitutability of goods. Under this assumption, an increase in the price of one good necessarily implies an increase in the demand for other goods: no two goods are considered as complementary. For example, in the real world an *increase* in the price of automobiles (which causes fewer new cars to be sold) might lead to a *decrease* in the sales of automobile tires (new tire sales being tied to new car sales). But under Wald's restrictive assumption an increase in the automobile price also *must increase* the demand for tires. Four decades later, Hugo Sonnenschein (1973) showed that it is absolutely impossible to eliminate multiple equilibrium solutions for a Walrasian system, because the functions of net demand are not linear or monotonic. Multiple equilibriums can and do exist, which leaves a place for chance, or more exactly, *for the effects of collective perceptions and choices,* in the determination of equilibrium levels of output and prices.

Problems of convergence and the supposed coordination of an auctioneer. Another problem area, separate from the existence of a single or multiple equilibrium set of outputs and prices, is the question of how the equilibrium is established. How, indeed, does one concretely depict the process of price adjustments that cause markets? Walras posits an "auctioneer" who is given the responsibility of modifying prices as a function of imbalances observed.

That is, the auctioneer increases prices when demand is excessive and lowers prices when there is an excess supply. This is Walrasian *tâtonnement* (a creeping, or gradual, adjustment process). This fiction raises two more questions. First, does the *tâtonnement* process lead to a convergence between supply and demand? The answer is no. An auctioneer who is trying to create market equilibrium by *tâtonnement* has no assurance of hitting on a vector leading to price equilibrium. This can only happen by reverting back to the restrictive assumption of gross substitutability of goods (cf. Wald 1936, and Arrow, Hurwicz, and Block 1959). In fact, the process becomes extremely complex as soon as we take into consideration the interactions between the different markets:

the modification of the price of good x, in order to correct an imbalance in the market for x, causes at the same time a modification in the price and supply conditions prevailing in all the other markets. All the other prices have to be revised, but each revision may in turn require all other prices (e.g., price in the market for x) to be revised yet again!

Which brings us to the second question. Does an "auctioneer" in fact exist? Obviously not. No one has ever met an auctioneer with a putative interest in the equilibrium of all markets. Indeed, the very process would require such heightened acuity and such vast quantities of information that it is hard to see how any one person, or even an institution, could play this role. Plainly, the assumption of an auctioneer is incompatible with the type of economy that Walras says he is analyzing: a *decentralized market economy,* where every participant can trade spontaneously and freely with neighbors, without going through some centralized office of price and supply coordination.

In the real world, a decentralized economy deviates significantly from the Walrasian model. Agents who have only imperfect information set prices on the basis of strategic or historical criteria. The concrete *intentions* that accompany the determination of prices are in general entirely independent of the objective of causing markets to clear. As soon as information and competition are imperfect, as when states control prices or monopolies control markets, a simple concrete price may have many dimensions: asking prices, limit prices, discriminating prices, and so on. Transactions may therefore occur at "false prices" (sometimes referred to as the nonmarket clearing price), which can lead to *non-Walrasian equilibriums.* The study of non-Walrasian equilibriums brings us to *disequilibrium theory*—a misnomer, since accounting identities are respected in this theory. Its principles are as follows: in the absence of the canceling out of all excess demands in the fashion described by Walras, certain market agents are rationed: they find no counterpart for their supply or demand. They must then ration their activity on other markets, causing new tensions to appear. In the absence of an auctioneer to regulate the price system with precision, generalized situations of *disequilibrium* can become established and last for long periods of time. We will see that such an approach is useful for a non-Walrasian Walrasian interpretation of Keynes. This contradictory jargon is necessary because it is explicit: the interpretation is Walrasian because it focuses on the interaction of markets, as Walras advocated, and non-Walrasian because transaction prices do not conform to the theory of equilibrium advanced by Walras.

Problems of pure economics. The third problem area of Walrasian economics concerns the organization of firms and entrepreneurs. This is what we mean by "pure economics." It brings us back to the *organization of production inside economic sectors* and, as we will see, the question of returns to scale, as has been discussed earlier with Marshall. In 1874 Walras proposed the simplifying assumption that production is carried out at a constant cost. That is, a linear relationship exists between the output of a good and costs: for example, if producing one shoe costs one dollar, then producing twenty shoes costs twenty dollars. But this assumption eliminates from the beginning all possibility of conducting a detailed analysis of the organization of firms. If the same production cost prevails regardless of sector organization, it makes no difference whether one large firm supplies the whole sector of economic activity or numerous minifirms produce, each one, an infinitesimal part of the sector's total output. Any intermediate number of firms is also possible. In a Walrasian universe, the size of the firms engaged in production is perfectly indeterminate.

This remark leads us to ask about the status of the entrepreneur: what are the purpose and role of a business executive when the status of the firm itself, its existence, and its objectives are indeterminate? Walras has no answer to this question. He understood, though, that abandoning the assumption of constant production costs would allow him, at least in part, to find an answer: excess profits, or differential profits between firms, appear as soon as we assume a differential rate of return. This differential gives entrepreneurs a function in the model, because each one will seek the best way to organize production so as to achieve the excess profit. Even so, Walras hits roadblocks to the coherence of his theory: to whom should surplus profits be redistributed? How do we envision profit rates separate from the equilibrium profit rate? And can these conditions last? The absence of a temporal dimension in Walras's theory of general equilibrium prevented his making any progress in answering these and related questions.

Irving Fisher, Time, and Money in the Theory of General Equilibrium

Time and money are the two major elements needing integration into general equilibrium theory. The need was well recognized, and many efforts were made. Without doubt, Irving Fisher (1867–1947) made one of the most interesting attempts. In his own writings, Keynes often used this American contemporary as a kind of theoretical interlocutor. After writing a doctoral thesis in 1892 that focused on general equilibrium, Irving Fisher devoted himself to the analysis of money and capital.

Money in the Theory of General Equilibrium

We turn first to where Walras left the question of money. At the end of his *Elements of Pure Economics*, money is presented as an addendum to the study of capital and productive services. According to Walras, the purpose of money (as, indeed, all capital goods) was to provide an advance service. It allows producers to pay the costs of production before the goods are in fact produced and sold. This treatment of money as a good in general equilibrium is therefore tied explicitly to a *temporal gap:* money theoretically allows producers to bridge the lapse of time that must pass before markets can clear. In Walras's universe, money exists *outside the equilibrium.* We will find this reasoning picked up, notably, in Robert Clower's interpretation of Keynesian theory.

In the Walrasian static equilibrium, nonetheless, money in effect disappears and goods are exchanged against goods. Walras supposes that money is not held for its own sake, but desired only because it satisfies the need to carry out transactions. In equilibrium, therefore, money can only be the reciprocal of real exchanges of goods, which are themselves predetermined by the interlocking system of relative prices. The "neutrality of money" in the Walrasian system—its inability to affect the exchange of real goods—is therefore guaranteed in advance by the a priori assumption that money has no value in itself. Therefore, Walras leaves money balances out of the utility function. Transactions in money are therefore balanced out—effectively set at zero—in equilibrium conditions, because economic agents are assumed to have no utility value in holding a stock of money. Mathematically, the introduction of money to the Walrasian system turns into the addition of a supplementary good and therefore of a new equilibrium equation to the whole series (see above, p. 61):

$$E_{n+1}(p_1, \ldots, p_k, \ldots, p_n) = 0.$$

This time, we count n unknowns with $(n + 1 - 1)$ independent equations. The introduction of money adds an equation, whereas Walras's law allows us to subtract one out (see above, p. 62). There are n equations and *n* unknowns; the addition of an explicit monetary sector permits the determination, for a given stock of money, of the *total* n *absolute prices of the system*: that is, the determination of $n + 1$ prices, where the price of money is 1. However, Irving Fisher specifies a more precise form of this excess demand function in his *Purchasing Power of Money* (1911).

In his own famous equation of exchange, Fisher does not stop at reformulating the classical dichotomy between real and monetary exchange. His theory followed his own careful study of the market. That is, he did not derive a rigid formula from a purely theoretical starting point. Working from careful statistical studies that he himself had conducted, he reformulated the *quantity theory of money* and confirmed Walras's view. Fisher defines the demand for money as:

$$M^d = (1/v) \sum_{i=1}^{n} P_i Q_i$$

The demand for money is proportional to the sum of all transactions, that is, the sum of all $P_i Q_i$. But money demand is also affected by money's velocity of circulation, shown as v, which corresponds to the number of times the means of payment can be reused in exchange. If money (such as a bill) passes five times from one person to another as these people buy and sell, only one-fifth as much money will be needed in circulation. Moreover, this money demand exists in relationship to a supply of money M^S that is supposed exogenous (M). This gives the market equilibrium, or Walrasian net demand, as:

$$E_{n+1}(P_1, \ldots, P_k, \ldots, P_n) = (1/v) \sum_{i=1}^{n} P_i Q_i - M = 0.$$

Breaking down the sum of all transactions into an index of all transaction prices, P, and into an index of the volume of all transactions, Q, we get Fisher's classic exchange equation:

$$PQ = Mv.$$

Fisher's equation of exchange is therefore shown here as the $n + 1$th equation of Walrasian system of exchange. It is the equilibrium equation for the money market. Let us note that in invoking Walras's law, this equation may also be derived from the equilibrium of the n other markets. It is often considered therefore as the $n + 1$th equation that has to be eliminated because of its link to the system's other equations. Nonetheless, even outside the market clearing process, the Fisher equation remains true: it has to be considered as a simple equality of sales and purchases (as already defined), an accounting identity among all the agents in the economy. That identity includes the central bank, which offers money for use in transactions. The equation therefore permits a simple way of calculating v as a ratio between the sum of all transactions and the stock of money as conventionally defined.

The equation of exchange is therefore always true. For Fisher, it does not need further theoretical justification; it can simply be used as a tool. Here we will simplify Fisher's analysis considerably.[2] In the long term, the value Q is considered as fixed exogenously by initial goods and factors of production. Also in the long term, the value v is considered determined by the institutional conditions of the banking system. *In the long run, variations in the supply of money can only affect the general price level.* In the equation, the only variable capable of reacting to a variation in M is P, and only P. The necessary condition for this conclusion to hold is a constant velocity of money circulation, v. In this respect, Fisher closely studied the customs and practices of banking systems, concluding that their tendency to put money deposits back into circulation with a constant velocity, v, was usually stable. After many analyses of events in which v and q undergo transitory change, Fisher ended up supporting a *flexible quantitative law,* which links the inflation rate *in the long term* to the growth rate of the monetary stock. "Flexible" means there is some wiggle room in the theory. A *rigid quantitative law* postulates the same relationship between the quantity of money and prices without any variation whatsoever; it considers the inflationary effect of an increase in M to be immediate. As we shall see, Keynes will pick up on Fisher's line of inquiry. More precisely, he will question how sensitive v is to the interest rate.

Time in General Equilibrium Theory: The Loanable Funds Market

Fisher made another crucial contribution to economic analysis: time. Should this contribution be distinguished from the equation of exchange?

Through the equation, money is already closely linked to the question of time—the time it takes for markets to clear. We nonetheless want to call attention to a second dimension of time in conditions of general equilibrium: Fisher's innovative theory of *interperiod (intertemporal) choice*. This intertemporal choice implies a time period longer than Walras's *tâtonnement*.[3]

More precisely, it is a period *between* two market equilibriums. Walras's notion of *tâtonnement* implies a period of time in which price adjustments occur, as part of his concept of equilibrium. Fisher adds to Walras's *tâtonnement* a second notion: the period between two *different* levels of equilibrium.

By way of example, we might consider the world economy in 1973, in which Walrasian *tâtonnement* was part of the ongoing process of economic equilibrium. In 1977 we had *another* Walrasian *tâtonnement,* adjusting prices at a new equilibrium level: one in which oil prices were four times higher than in 1973, due to the actions of Organization of the Petroleum Exporting Countries (OPEC). During 1974, 1975, and 1976, the world went through the difficult period of adjustment between the two equilibrium levels of 1973 and 1977. The period of adjustment between two *different* levels of equilibrium is the concept of time that Fisher adds to the Walrasian system. So the questions Fisher raises concern the "long period" and involve saving and investment decisions.

Fisher's interest rate and capital market theories are therefore crucial to understanding Keynes's research. The dramatic shift between the equilibrium levels of the world economy in the 1920s and of the Great Depression in the 1930s required a focus on how and why a transition occurs between two equilibrium states.

Fisher published his *Theory of Interest* in 1930, but his analysis is already delineated in his earlier *Rate of Interest: Its Nature, Determination, and Relation to Economic Phenomena* (1907). His goal is to extend the study of general equilibrium to *intertemporal choices*. Breaking with Walras, who, to do this, tried to conserve the disaggregated structure of his model, with n goods and x agents, Fisher, conscious of the complexity of the effects to be studied, decided to simplify: he proceeded as if there were only one "universal good" that was to be produced, consumed, saved, and invested. (This abstraction is analogous to the *aggregate output* of modern macroeconomics, where the national income Y is a weighted average of n goods, which can be used as much for consumption as investment.) Individual choices determine how this "universal good" is produced and consumed over time, which is what we mean by saving and investment. The intertemporal allocation of this universal good occurs in a particular place, which we call the capital markets, or loanable fund markets. In these markets, Fisher distinguishes between two types of choices: savings choices that are affected by tastes, and investment choices that are governed by technologies. To summarize:

- The *savings choices*, which *supply capital*, come from the behavior of private agents who freely establish a personal, intertemporal consumption plan over their lifetime. Savings are, in this way of looking at things, a means to transfer consumption from the present to some future consumption moment. The preferred argument is that economic agents, or savers, compare *their preference for immediate consumption* (a psychological choice linked to their impatience) with the *yield on their savings:* the real interest rate. The supply of capital increases as a function of the interest rate: the higher it is, the more saving is rewarded, and the more private agents are induced to save. The yield on savings compensates them for not consuming in the present.
- On the other hand, *investment*, or the *demand for capital goods*, proceeds from an intertemporal allocation of production decisions. Investment is the choice to produce a bit less of consumption goods today, in order to be able to produce more of them tomorrow. The technological efficiency of capital goods plays a determining role in this decision. More precisely, the arbitrage decision (between investing or not) is, according to Fisher, controlled by the comparison agents make between the *investment opportunity* that measures the physical productivity of capital (easily measurable because in this model there is only one good, which is at once input and output), and the unit cost of the investment, which is the real interest rate. The demand for capital is a decreasing function of the rate of interest. The rate of interest reflects the cost of mobilizing invested capital: an increase in the interest rate will have the effect of eliminating investment projects whose productivity is inferior.

In the classical assumptions, in both cases, economic agents are only sensitive to the *real* interest rate. They have no *monetary illusion,* because they are assumed to know how to distinguish the general increase in prices from the evolution of the nominal rate of interest. (At low rates of interest and inflation, the real interest rate is approximately equal to the nominal interest rate minus the inflation rate). As Figure 2.6 indicates, the right rate of interest (such as $r = r^*$) is the one that brings supply and demand into balance. For any given group of people, the

Figure 2.6 **Fisher's Capital Market**

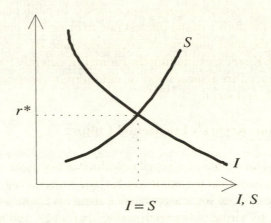

r = real interest rate; r^* = equilibrium real interest rate, I = investment, S = saving.

desire to consume immediately and the opportunity to invest confront each other as opposing goals in the capital markets. Fisher's theory identifies the interest rate as the key variable: it balances the desire to consume with the opportunity to invest.

Fisher's analysis is therefore clearly integrated into the general Walrasian equilibrium model. Savings and investment, treated as macroeconomic concepts, are analyzed in the context of a particular market that is nonetheless interdependent with all the other sectors, though Figure 2.6 isolates the capital market from the markets for other goods in order to illustrate a point. And, like Walras's work, Fisher's message is on the whole reassuring: price adjustments, their perfect flexibility, guarantee that the economic plans and activities of different agents will be compatible.

But Fisher has made an important theoretical jump: the equilibrium he envisions is *intertemporal,* in that it now entails many successive periods; moreover, in each period, markets clear. This is the first formulation of a *temporary* general equilibrium (at any instant *t*), of which the mainspring is the continuous adjustment of capital markets and the flexibility of the rate of interest. This emphasis on the role of time in equilibrium conditions is a critical starting point for Keynes's own views. Fisher would greatly influence Keynes. For example, the concept of investment opportunity developed by Fisher is very close to Keynes's own marginal efficiency of capital, as Keynes himself stated. However, Keynes would later dispute some of Fisher's theses. In particular, he would cast doubts on the ability of the interest rate to bring into perfect balance, all by itself, the total universe of decisions made by investors about the future. For Keynes, estimating the future is inherently too complex to be easily reduced to a succession of equilibrium positions over periods, $t + 1, t + 2$, and so on.

Conclusion: Keynes's Intellectual Culture

The ideas that we have surveyed constitute economists' *intellectual culture* in this historical period. It was Keynes's intellectual culture as well. Though he evinced some ambivalence about his choice of career, Keynes remained, by virtue of his upbringing, his friends, and his activities, an eminent member of the community of economists. As his letters abundantly testify, he knew that community's debates and participated in them. In this respect, the 1930s constituted a crucial developmental juncture for economic thinking: methods were being standardized, and the first great theoretical results were either already established or on their way to being so. Research was increasingly oriented to extending economic reasoning, and to assess the validity of that reasoning, whether by internal or external standards. Money and time appear as the key issues of both the partial and general equilibrium approaches. Table 2.1 captures the advantages and problems of the two approaches.

This simple table summarizes the preoccupations of economists during the 1930s. To some extent, these issues also help us understand some of Keynes's insights. From the Walrasian approach, Keynes will take up, as will others, the necessity of looking at markets as an interconnected whole. Most especially, the market for goods and services must be considered in relation to the markets for money and securities. Hicks, who sought to make Walras better known in Britain, would emphasize this aspect of Keynes's contribution: the IS-LM model, invented by Hicks in 1937, is the strongest possible example of this focus on the interdependence of markets for money and goods. However, Keynes would never abandon the Marshallian tradition. To compensate for general equilibrium theory's weakest point, its fictional auctioneer who directs prices to convergence on an equilibrium vector, Keynes drew on the Cambridge tradition. If we do not wish to negate the concept of dynamic equilibrium by a fiction, we must have a concrete principle by which prices are

Table 2.1

Summary of Marshall's and Walras's Price Theories

	Advantages	Disadvantages
Marshallian approach	Describes dynamics of price adjustment periods	Interactions between markets not taken into account
Walrasian approach	Attempts to analyze market interactions interdependence	Deficient description of price convergence dynamics (auctioneer)

determined. Whatever this principle may be, it most assuredly must *operate through time.* The theoretical necessity of a precise description of sector dynamics is reintroduced.

The fictitious auctioneer therefore does not determine prices a priori. Prices can even be *false,* that is, determined in some manner other than zeroing out all the excess demand equations of the Walrasian system. Abandoning the hypothesis of the Walrasian auctioneer leads to a new series of problems that, in fact, are typical of the whole thrust of Keynes's work. The chapters that follow will focus on *uncertainty* and *money* as Keynes's principal concerns. For the moment, we emphasize the logical coherence of focusing on these two subjects, given the existence of false prices. The possibility of carrying out transactions under conditions of false prices leads, first of all, to the problem of uncertainty. In the absence of market clearing, a certain number of transactions that economic agents have counted on happening do not, in fact, happen. Some goods are demanded but not produced; others are produced but not bought. Even worse, as we have seen, scarcity, or rationing, in one market can have a domino effect that produces more rationing in still other markets, which in turn creates new uncertainty.

If transactions can occur outside of market-clearing equilibrium conditions, *money* comes into play in a way that classical and neoclassical theories rule out. Money is forced into a new role. It regulates the market and is the balance held—positive or negative—by market agents who have been on the winning or losing side of rationing in markets that fail to clear. To establish this, we need only consider the accounting balance of purchases and sales that market agents have in conditions of equilibrium, and disequilibrium, in Table 2.2.

In the first type of account (the hypothetical barter economy in equi-

Table 2.2

Transaction Balances and Market Clearing

Transaction balances in a barter or equilibrium, economy		Transaction balances for a money economy in disequilibrium (false prices)	
Purchases	Sales	Purchases	Sales
All real purchases (desired purchases are in fact realized)	All real sales (desired sales are in fact realized)	All effective purchases (but all anticipated purchases may not be realized)	All real sales (but all anticipated sales may not be realized)
Balance: zero		Balance: unknown. A nonzero balance must be held as money	

librium, shown as two columns on the left), all the sales that are foreseen satisfy all the purchases that are foreseen. Money is therefore not demanded as something for its own sake. It is used only as an intermediary in the exchange process. In equilibrium, therefore, money's role in the economy is *necessarily* neutral. The final balance of all transactions is therefore shown as zero. On the other hand, in the second type of account (the money economy shown as two columns on the right, where prices are false and the economy is in disequilibrium), transactions made with false prices have caused certain sales or purchases to fail to be realized. The variable that allows the accounts to be balanced is *money*. The existence of transactions in nonequilibrium conditions therefore implies, from one period to another, that the accounts of economic agents do not balance, unless their cash holdings are changing to make the accounts do so.

Money is therefore reintroduced, for example, by Clower (1969), as an adjustment principle for transactions that have failed to clear. Money is the counterweight of disequilibriums in the markets for real goods. Two points may be made about this. First, we may discern in this role of money one of Walras's earlier intuitions. For Walras had envisioned money as relevant to conditions outside of equilibrium. But, as we have seen, he abandoned his own speculations about money because he refused to consider transactions under conditions of false prices: the auctioneer serves to guarantee true pricing. Keynes, on the contrary, proposes an alternative theory of price determination: in reality, entrepreneurs take the place of the auctioneer and set—or at least influence—the prices of their goods. When entrepreneurs set their own prices, market clearing cannot be assumed.

Second, money and uncertainty, though presented separately, now appear to be intrinsically linked. The risk that expected transactions might not in fact occur introduces at once both uncertainty and money. These two notions are completely intertwined throughout Keynes's work, though their relationship is not fully resolved: is it the existence of money, which has no intrinsic value, that causes uncertainty? Or is it uncertainty that crystallizes into the form of money and then gains value as "refuge" for unbalanced transactions?

In reality, both insights are valid, because they share a common cause: market failure. The close relationship between these two insights in turn emphasizes the aspect of money that is most directly linked to uncertainty: its *liquidity*.

Notes

1. Arguably Walras's equations should have been written as inequalities, in order to consider the case of abundant goods whose price falls to zero and which cannot even be given away. However, as a practitioner of the "dismal science" of economics, Walras (like most other economists) focused exclusively on the case of scarce goods.

2. We will not break down VM into $v'M'$ and $V''M''$," or cash + checking deposit transactions.

3. In Walras's theory, all trades occur in equilibrium, so *tâtonnement* must occur in a hypothetical "virtual" time.

3

Keynes Before the *General Theory*

Keynes's major work is the *General Theory of Employment, Interest, and Money*. Published in 1936, the *General Theory* has for more than half a century defined Keynesian thought as an autonomous current of economic analysis. Before 1936, Keynes wrote and published many other books, articles, and pamphlets. In this chapter, we focus on two of Keynes's most important earlier works: the *Treatise on Money* and the *Treatise on Probability*.

The two treatises, particularly in introductory works, are rarely summarized together, a practice that neglects major aspects of Keynes's thought. The two works are not easily accessible. They were written for a university and professional readership. Moreover, as Keynes himself acknowledged, the two treatises both suffered from flawed presentations, which does not encourage new readers. Nonetheless, the earlier books both throw a good deal of light on the rest of Keynes's work. They do this at all levels: in their choice of subjects, in the concepts they present, and even in their faults. Our presentation will be clearer if we reverse chronological order and begin with the *Treatise on Money*.

The *Treatise on Money*

Written toward the end of the 1920s and published in 1930, the *Treatise on Money* is a work of "monetary theory," to use the author's words. With this label Keynes hoped to distinguish the massive two-volume book from the raft of lesser works that he had also written in the 1920s. These were almost always more polemical and usually less well thought out; a brief overview of this period has already been given in Chapter 1. The *Treatise on Money* is a marathon intellectual effort. Its initial conception and writing occupied Keynes from 1924 through 1929, and indeed, was his major project from just after his *Tract on Monetary Reform* up to the writing of the *General Theory* in its earliest stages.

During these years Keynes wrestled with profound theoretical problems. The resulting intellectual conflicts may have weakened the overall message of the *Treatise*. As he confessed in September 1930, in a letter to his mother, "Artistically it is a failure—I have changed my mind too much during the course of it for it to be a proper unity" (*CW* 13:176).

Keeping in mind Keynes's own misgivings, we will not summarize the work in all its complex meandering and dead ends. We shall instead emphasize one part of the *Treatise:* its macroeconomic analysis of cyclical disturbances in general equilibrium. We emphasize this part of the *Treatise* because in retrospect it offers some very useful insights into the thinking behind the later *General Theory*.

The Analysis of Economic Fluctuations

The macroeconomics of the *Treatise* focuses on the links between money and cyclical disturbances of an economy. Cyclical disturbances affect general price levels and the level of economic activity. The Cambridge equation is the departure point for Keynes's investigation. More exactly, the economist worried about the *indirect effect* of the Cambridge quantitative schema: the paradox of assuming, following an increase in the money supply, that the supply of goods stays stable while lower interest rates spur additional investment.

The Paradox of the Indirect Effect

As we have already seen with Pigou (see previous chapter), the quantitative relationship between the stock of money and the price level depends on two key theoretical assumptions. One is the *real balance effect*, which describes how monetary excesses can either be put into circulation or withdrawn. The second is the hypothesis of a *fixed supply of goods*, which allows one to easily demonstrate the inflationary effect of increased demand on a constant level of output. In the *Treatise on Money*, Keynes casts doubts on, but eventually accepts, these two theoretical assumptions.

Keynes reviews and then recasts the question of the real balance effect by introducing two distinct forms of bank balances. *Cash deposits* serve the transaction motive of economic agents, while *savings deposits* serve to transfer purchasing power from the present to the future.

In short, the two major institutional ways for keeping money in the bank corresponded to the two principal reasons for the demand for money. Here we already see a distinction that Keynes will rework later, when he will argue that money is held either to meet transaction needs or speculative needs. However, it is only in the later *General Theory* that Keynes will challenge the very notion of a stable demand for money. In the *Treatise on Money,* the demand for money may vary according to the type of deposit, but this distinction ultimately becomes useless. It is useless because Keynes accepts the idea of constant holdings of real money regardless of the particular form of deposit. Keynes has two values of k in the sense defined by Pigou, the cash deposit and the savings deposit, but neither varies in the long term. The ratio of cash to savings deposits also does not vary.

Regarding the *fixed supply of goods,* Keynes zeroes in on a contradiction in the "indirect effect" of the Cambridge quantity theory of money. Just how can it be that a fixed supply of goods, which is what causes prices to rise, can exist at the same time that lower interest rates are supposedly spurring additional investment? The two assumptions are logically incompatible. Investment, by definition, modifies productive capacity. Therefore, investment must modify, in the end, the level of supply in the economy.

Inexplicably, Keynes discovers this contradiction, discusses it, and then incorporates it into his assumptions! In the *Treatise,* he simply cannot break with the quantity theory of money. Like others, such as Fisher and Pigou, confronted with the indirect effect of boosting investment, he preferred, at this time, to find a way around the paradox rather than to renounce the quantity theory of money. In a way, this evasion is the principal goal of the *Treatise on Money.* Let us see how Keynes worked around the problem.

The Credit Cycle

The indirect effect leads to a cycle linked to variations in private investment. The orthodox position, which Keynes adopted, must show exactly how the increase in production is temporary. After monetary stimulation to the economy, the cycle will inevitably bring production back to

Figure 3.1 **The Credit Cycle**

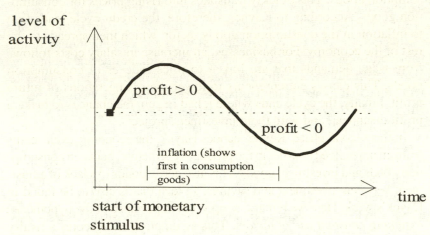

the level that existed before the stimulation. Figure 3.1 illustrates Keynes's thinking. Two periods are distinguished therein.

First phase: growth and entrepreneurial profits. The growth phase of the cycle begins immediately after the act of monetary creation. As predicted by Pigou's indirect effect, banks respond to the easy availability of money by letting interest rates fall. The price of bank credit falls below the internal rate of return on capital employed in businesses. Entrepreneurs see better prospects for making a profit. Investment is stimulated, and the first phase of the cycle is under way.

At this point, Keynes borrows an idea from Wicksell (whom we will discuss later). The disparity between the bank rate of interest and the internal rate of return on investment projects initiates the cycle. Nonetheless, Keynes insists on adding a specific causal factor: *entrepreneurial profits.* It is the increased margin of profit, made possible by the disparity of rates, that breathes into the economy its own dynamic.

Second phase: return to the point of departure, and inflation caused by insufficient consumption goods. The growth in investment causes factors of production previously destined for sectors that produce consumption goods to be turned instead to the needs of sectors that produce capital goods. But, as soon as this is done, *assuming the total use of these re-*

sources remains constant, there must appear a relative scarcity of consumption goods. This quickly translates into rising prices for consumption goods. According to Keynes, therefore, the credit cycle leads first to inflation in the consumption goods sector, which then spreads to the rest of the economy. For businesses, an increase in salary costs follows from wage demands that are linked to price indexes of consumption goods. This causes entrepreneurs to lower their expectations of future profit. Finally, the cycle ends where it had begun: the chances to make a profit disappear, and with them investment projects.

In this second phase, Keynes echoes Hayek: the economic cycle stems from an unresolved conflict in the productive structure, between consumption goods and investment goods. This also corresponds to a lack of adjustment between investment and savings, an idea that is also to be found in Hayek's work. Here we remark, simply, the importance of the hypothesis: *assuming constant use of factors.* This assumption underscores a rivalry between the economy's two great sectors (consumption and investment) in obtaining the factor goods they need. This rivalry leads to the necessity of inflation and therefore of a return to the beginning of the cycle.

The credit cycle must, therefore, lead to inflation. The monetary stimulus, even if it creates a short-term increase in investment, is fundamentally useless. This is Keynes's opinion at this point. Let us see how he supports his position using mathematics.

Mathematics and the Treatise on Money

This detour into Keynes's formal mathematical statement is intended to clarify his reasoning in the *Treatise,* but even more importantly, the road he took to get to the *General Theory.* It was, in fact, an error found in his accounting model that made Keynes feel the need to develop new ideas that he would use later. For the sake of clarity, the notation used below follows contemporary practice rather than Keynes's notation. We have also simplified the model presented in the *Treatise.*[1]

Definitions, Accounting Equations, the Fundamental Equation

The index of the general price level P and that of total production Q are written as follows:

$$PQ = (P_c Q_c) + (P_i Q_i).$$

The value of the aggregate production PQ proceeds from two sectors, one for the price and quantity of consumption goods ($P_c Q_c$), the other for investment goods ($P_i Q_i$). The value of total investment ($P_i Q_i$) may be represented as I, giving

$$PQ = (P_c Q_c) + I. \tag{1}$$

By using I to represent the value of investment ($P_i Q_i$), we deliberately leave out the financial process. Businesses' need for finance is directly linked to the need to buy investment goods. Financiers turn these actions into paper titles, or securities. For simplicity, we leave out the process of financial intermediation that in any case does not change the reasoning.

The equilibrium condition of resource use among *businesses* can be written as follows:

$$R + \pi = PQ. \tag{2}$$

For Keynes, the total revenues of businesses, represented by PQ, can be broken down into normal revenue, R, and exceptional profits, π. The concept of surplus profits, π, is derived from Marshall (as with the excess profits on fish in the previous chapter). The term "normal," applied to R, indicates revenue that is defined without regard to short-term variations. The term R is therefore a theoretical object, meaningful over the long period.

The equilibrium condition of *households* and how they use their receipts can be written as follows:

$$(P_c Q_c) + S = R. \tag{3}$$

Households can employ the distributed revenue R in two ways: they can consume it ($P_c Q_c$), or they can save it (S). If they save it, they will be putting their funds into the market for capital goods.

Equations (1) and (3) give what the *Treatise on Money* calls the "fundamental equation":

$$PQ = R + I - S. \tag{4}$$

This equation is the basis for Keynes's arguments as presented in the *Treatise*.

Results of the Fundamental Equation

The first result is that the presence of excess profits corresponds strictly to a disparity between investment and savings. From equations (4) and (2) it follows that

$$\pi = I - S.$$

This result may be compared to the description of the *credit cycle*. The beginning of the cycle, the reason it exists, is the appearance of a surplus profit (an exceptional profit that exceeds the normal rate of return on capital). The surplus profit is written $\pi > 0$. But this effect has an immediate corollary: it corresponds strictly to an excess of financing needs (denoted by I) over the total ability of households to save (denoted by S): $I > S$. The economic cycle is therefore intrinsically linked to an imbalance between savings and investment.

The second result of the fundamental equation is this: the general price level is explained by the imbalance between I and S, as a corollary of the credit cycle. From equation (4) we can deduce:[2]

$$P = \frac{R}{Q} + \frac{I-S}{Q}. \tag{5}$$

In (5) Q is fixed by the use of factors of production; R is determined by principle of a *normal* revenue from these factors. A cyclical disequilibrium between I and S leads to inflation when I is greater than S: in the equation above, P increases as the value of I increases. Everything seems to indicate that the disequilibrium in the credit market is resolved, not by an adjustment of the rate of interest, but by an increase in prices: it is inflation that provides the adjustment mechanism for disequilibrium.

So it appears that Keynes's fundamental equation is nothing less than a modified *quantity theory* equation. It explains the increase in prices through an unusual mechanism: surplus profits. By expressing R in its monetary form, we get, in Fisher's way of writing,

$$R = Mv.$$

The fundamental equation, in these terms, becomes:

$$PQ = Mv + \pi.$$

Here we see the whole purpose of introducing π into quantitative theory. In the short run, $\pi \neq 0$, and an excess profit is inserted in the relationship between M and P, which weakens their relationship. In the long run, that is to say, in the second period of the cycle, $\pi = 0$. In this case, the excess profit ends up where it began, and the causal relationship between M and P is shown to be complete.

The Fundamental Equation: An Error?

Clearly, the variable π indicates a disturbance: Keynes is trying to model an economy that is *out of equilibrium.* That is, he is trying to capture the moment before market clearing, and especially the clearing of financial markets, has been able to take place. This is the means that Keynes found to envision an economy undergoing cyclical activity and to observe its return to equilibrium.

However, the definition of an excess profit is problematic. It is at once nonzero and yet somehow distinguishable from "true" or "ordinary" revenues. The concept raises questions of logical coherence. The problem is illustrated in Figure 3.2, where we may compare the separate employment and resource accounts of households and businesses. In Figure 3.2, the superscripts d and s show the market form that each accounting value takes: d = demand, s = supply. As for I and S, after they have been processed by the banking system, I will correspond to a supply of securities for sale on financial markets, and S will correspond to the demand for them.

The expenditures (or outlays in business terminology) made by businesses do *not* get entered as "receipts" in the accounting of households. This may be considered, within the reasoning of this model, as a conceptual error. There are only two explicit agents in this two-sector model (finance as a distinct agent has not been taken into account). It follows that the outlays of the business sector must *necessarily* be identical to the receipts of the household sector, and vice versa. Yet Keynes does not maintain the identity of receipts and outlays. In other words, in this model, Walras's law is not respected. By adding the sum of all net demands, we get

$$P_c^* (Q_c^d - Q_c^s) + S - I = (R - S) - (R + \pi - I) + S - I = -\pi \ldots (^1 \neq 0).$$

The sum of the net demands is nonzero and instead equals the absolute value of π, which is the sum of the initial accounting error.

Two explanations are possible for this error. It might have been a

Figure 3.2 **Double Entry Bookkeeping: Keynes's Error**

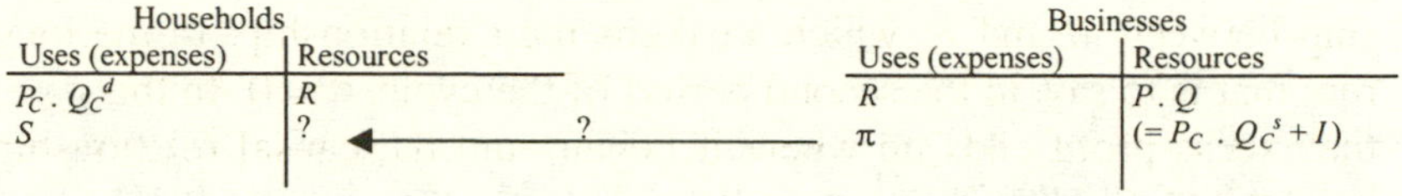

Households					Businesses	
Uses (expenses)	Resources				Uses (expenses)	Resources
$P_c \cdot Q_c^d$	R				R	$P \cdot Q$
S	? ⟵ ?			π		$(= P_c \cdot Q_c^s + 1)$

voluntary error. Keynes might have invented this error to escape Walras's law so as to outline a sequential process of reasoning, where the economy in disequilibrium might be explicitly observed. This is the position of Cartelier (1995). In this view, the mechanism π, and its nonzero variations in value, give life to the model.

Or it was an error pure and simple. Keynes's colleague, the economist Richard Kahn, observed, in this respect, that the concept of surplus profit should be integrated into the revenue distributed. It should not be distinguished from R. In this case, equation (2) is replaced by equation (2′):

$$R = PQ. \tag{2′}$$

And the fundamental equation (4) becomes (4′):

$$I = S \tag{4′}$$

This is in fact the position that Keynes will subsequently take in the *General Theory*.

Absent a perturbation value provided by π, the mathematics of the *Treatise* gives a model of the economy *in equilibrium*. It is exact and rigorous for a given moment, T, but is incapable of showing the succession of adjustments required so that this virtual or ideal moment T is actually reached. Keynes will later find, however, an alternative means to think about an economy *out of equilibrium* by distinguishing, in the *General Theory, expected* values from *realized* values. This new distinction, in Keynes's mind, seems to work perfectly as a substitute for the problematic introduction of π. Keynes explained himself:

> In my *Treatise on Money* the concept of *changes* in the excess of investment over saving, as there defined, was a way of handling changes in profit, though I did not in that book distinguish clearly between expected and realised results. . . . Thus the new argument, though (as I now think)

much more accurate and instructive, is essentially a development of the old. (*CW* 7:77–78; italics in original)

This discussion was not a mere afterthought. It is fundamental to understanding how Keynes's thought changed from the *Treatise on Money* to the *General Theory* and as such is part of the conclusions that follow.

Conclusion: From the Treatise on Money *to the* General Theory

Our study of the *Treatise* has focused on how Keynes's thinking developed before the *General Theory*. What elements of the *Treatise* did he have to give up? Moreover, once Keynes's thinking changed, was anything of value left in the *Treatise*?

What Premises Did Keynes Have to Give Up?

Abandoned Premise No. 1: The separation of excess profits from ordinary revenue.

Keynes accepted Kahn's criticism, discussed above. Five years later, the *General Theory* showed just how much he took Kahn's objections to heart. Changing his mind on this point caused Keynes no small inconvenience. He had to abandon the *Treatise*'s mathematics and modify the semantic content of almost all the ideas in it. Keynes seems to have rallied to a definition of revenue that included excess profits when they occurred. By doing so, he accepted the fundamental equation $I = S$ for realized values, even if expected values might be different.

Some have found this regrettable. By distinguishing expected values from realized values Keynes accepted, for realized values, the principle of analyzing them from an *equilibrium* perspective, rather than a *sequential* perspective. The sequential perspective sets out the different, successive phases of disequilibrium through which, in the real world, an economy must pass. Keynes's decision in this respect may have worked to limit the diversity of economic thought. Nonetheless, Keynes's own discussion of why he made these changes, as cited above, shows clearly enough that he intended to make a deliberate choice in favor of orthodox economic thinking. By extension, he opted for accounting rigor. It must be said that Kahn, while demolishing the structure of the *Treatise,* nonetheless provided some principles for a new one: the use of profits (and excess profits) not as a simple *expenditure* of businesses but as a *revenue* will permit the elaboration of a new mechanism that regulates disequilibriums. This brings us to our second point.

Abandoned Premise No. 2: The full employment of factors of production and the constancy of aggregate production.

If we are considering conditions in equilibrium and take into account the error of Abandoned Premise No. 1, above, then savings and investment are necessarily equal.

But how do we explain this equality? How do two sets of actors, households making savings and businesses making investments, adjust their respective behaviors so that their two activities are equal? In 1931 Kahn offered an answer: he developed the notion of the "multiplier," which makes the adjustment between the two values, I and S, depend on *variations of aggregate output.*

We will pursue the multiplier principle in the chapters that follow. To tie it to our discussion of profits and excess profits, we need only say that the multiplier is based on the idea of a strict equality between how businesses use their revenues and what resources in turn are at the disposal of households. Reintegrating π into R, and correcting Keynes's mistake, was a necessary step to invent the multiplier effect. Kahn in effect made a double contribution: he diagnosed the error and he proposed a solution. Moreover, the diagnosis and the solution are linked. The balance between resources and their uses mirrors the balance that must exist between the household sector and the business sector. In other words, Figure 3.2 is false because the right side of the diagram (businesses) and the left side (households) *must* be, in the aggregate, in balance, and discovering how balance is in fact realized was a new subject of research.

Keynes's post-*Treatise* distinction between the *expected* values of outlays and receipts and their ultimate *realized* values was at the crux of his later research. He was especially concerned with the impact of the *expected* on the *realized.* Another way of looking at this is that Keynes was on the verge of abandoning the hypothesis of constant aggregate output, as determined by the full employment of factors of production. In his new way of thinking, economic social reality would no longer be determined by a putative "natural equilibrium." This step was extremely radical. It far outweighed the conservative implications of accepting the orthodox equilibrium and accounting approach mentioned earlier.

Indeed, Kahn's criticism of Keynes's error in the *Treatise,* and Kahn's proposed multiplier effect, would prove a major stepping-stone in revealing the hidden errors of the famous classical assumptions. These assumptions were traditionally presented as simplifying and of no great consequence in economic analysis. The notion of *natural* income level, determined by the available factors (labor, capital, natural resources, etc.), was thereby challenged. By contrast, Kahn and his multiplier effect opened a new field of research: the explicit study of those mechanisms that determine the level of economic activity without regard to constraints imposed by factor endowments.

What Was Left of the Treatise?

Retained Premise No. 1: The adjustment of I and S is a core element of cyclical disturbances in the economy.

In spite of its errors, the *Treatise* was useful. By criticizing it, both Keynes and Kahn discovered principles that were fundamental to the *General Theory.* In fact, the *Treatise* posed the problem quite well: In the absence of sufficient flexibility in the interest rate, the adjustment of I and S requires large-scale fluctuations that suggest major macroeconomic consequences. Still, the answer to the problem remained questionable. In 1930, Keynes proposed the general level of prices P as the factor that adjusts an imbalance between I and S. This was seen in equation (5) above. In 1936, Keynes offered a different adjustment factor to account for at least part of the reaction to an imbalance between I and S. Using the multiplier effect, he argued that the overall level of economic activity Q must adjust the overall imbalance. (Y is usually preferred today and is used in Chapter 5 of this book.)

Retained Premise No. 2: Entrepreneurs play the major role in determining economic activity.

The *Treatise*'s focus on entrepreneurs and their activity itself merits a brief discussion. In this work, Keynes puts special emphasis on this particular group of agents. Their behavior and their reactions create alternating periods of economic stagnation and growth, also called crisis and expansion. The concept of excess profits (π) has at least this element of interest: it clearly points a finger at the central agent who determines the overall level of investment and, therefore, variations in levels of economic activity. In the *General Theory,* Keynes will again use this idea, only much more systematically. Entrepreneurs will emerge as the mainspring of adjustments between *I* and *S* in the economy. Moreover, the new distinction between expected values and realized values (invented in the *General Theory*) will allow Keynes to refine his views about entrepreneurial behavior. Entrepreneurs—their beliefs, their fears, and their resulting action and inaction—will become central to a view of the economic system that henceforth will be influenced by uncertainty at all levels.

This uncertainty, in fact, allows us to move to Keynes's *Treatise on Probability* and how it affected his thinking in the years before the *General Theory*.

The *Treatise on Probability*

Today, the *Treatise on Probability* is considered fundamental to understanding Keynes's work. There is widespread agreement that uncertainty plays a major role in his vision of economics. The *Treatise on Probability* stands out as an early masterpiece that must be considered by anyone who wants to understand Keynes's thinking about uncertainty.

The work was produced as a doctoral dissertation under the direction of A.N. Whitehead, a mathematician and philosopher. It was defended in 1909. After much rewriting, Keynes published the work in 1921. Keynes's thesis, here as in many other things, was at once audacious, original, and polemical. His goal was neither more nor less than to give a new foundation to thinking about probability. As a doctoral thesis and, later, as a book, the work provoked a wide range of responses. The book played an influential role in the thinking of probability theorists and mathematicians such as Frank P. Ramsey (1926), Leonard Savage (1954), and Rudolf Carnap (1950).

The Nature of Chance: The Impossibility of the "Frequentist Position"

The *Treatise on Probability* begins by arguing against an older notion of probability, called "frequentist." Frequentists believe that the probability of a given event in the future may be inferred from how often it has occurred in the past. Keynes's distinction between the *weight* and *probability* of a way of thinking is central to his line of argument.

The Urn Example: How We Experience Real Events, from Risk to Uncertainty

Keynes's main points about uncertainty were very neatly summed up by Georgescu-Roegen. Georgescu-Roegen (1958, 24) asks us to consider four examples, labeled e_1 through e_4, concerning four separate urns, U_1 through U_4. In his words:

> [L]et us consider the following evidence about urns containing balls, identical save for color:
>
> e_1 = in U_1, two-thirds of the balls are white and one-third are black;
>
> e_2 = the frequency of white in 3,426 independent extractions from U_2, was 2/3;
>
> e_3 = three independent extractions from U_3 resulted in two white and one black ball;
>
> e_4 = the urn U_4 contains some balls.

In each case, the real-world situation of an individual in front of an urn is identical: only the *information* about the urn is different. The four examples e_1 through e_4 describe a range that runs from *risk* to *uncertainty*. This terminology was put forward by the American economist and philosopher Frank Knight (1921). Knight suggested that the word *uncertainty* be reserved for situations that do not lend themselves to probabilistic calculations. The term *risk* should be reserved for situations in which chance plays a role, but probabilities can be calculated.

Clearly, the first two instances, e_1 and e_2, put a person in a condition of *risk*. A person trying to guess the color of a ball before pulling it out is in a situation governed by chance, but the chance can be calculated as a probability: e_1 is certain to offer a probability of 1/3 to pull out a white ball. Thousands of samples assure us that e_2 is almost as certain to offer a 1/3 probability of a white ball as e_1.

Instances e_3 and e_4, on the other hand, put us in a situation of *uncertainty*. The use of probability to estimate the chances of pulling out a red ball is arguable. E_3 offers more information than e_4, but even so, three samples do not establish a high degree of confidence in the composition of the next sample.

The real world generally, and economics in particular, are, according to Keynes, much more similar to the situation of e_4 than e_1. In fact, e_1 is much more typical of the contrived conditions of a laboratory than the real world, because in the laboratory chance conditions are specifically constructed. The range from e_2 to e_4 represents the conditions of daily life. Sometimes we seem to have repeated samples of information of apparently high reliability (e_2), but often, the scarcity of data weakens (e_3) or even prevents altogether (e_4) the ability to make any meaningful guess about the real world.

These distinctions allow Keynes to argue against the traditional arguments regarding probability, the frequentist position. In the frequentist view, probabilities are derived from repeated observations of an event and a calculation of its mathematical frequency. However, most of the time, daily life does not allow us to calculate a probability rigorously grounded on a large number of repeated experiences. Thus, even e_2, in the list above, is for the most part irrelevant. But, rather than invalidate probabilistic approaches, Keynes tries to improve on them with a highly original distinction: the difference between *probability* and *weight*.

The Distinction Between Probability and Weight

Let us observe the behavior of a person in the three urn examples in which information is available: e_1, e_2, and e_3. From e_1 to e_3, the probability that a person would use to estimate the chances of pulling out a white ball does not change. It remains 1/3 in each case. Nonetheless, the degree of confidence that we will give to each value will vary a great deal. In e_1, confidence in the calculation of probability is total; in e_2, confidence in the calculation of probability is very high. In e_3, however, confidence in the calculation of probability is very weak. In other words, whereas the inductive part of the probability, based on experience, does not change, the *weight* of this inductive proposition is extremely affected.

Keynes proposes the following distinction. The term *probability* describes probabilities of the first order, that is, those derived directly from observation. A new observation can either reduce our estimate of the probability of an event, or increase it. The term *weight,* by contrast, is reserved for second-order probabilities, those that indicate the *degree of confidence* in a probabilistic judgment. Confidence in a causal relationship between two events goes up with available information: as a result, w*eight* always increases with an increasing number of observations.

The distinction between weight and probability helps clarify the different degrees between *risk* and *uncertainty.* In e_1, guessing correctly the color of a ball pulled out of the urn is a risk but it is not uncertain. The *weight* of the probabilistic calculation is therefore at its maximum (or, in probability parlance, 1). In e_3, the weight is weak (close to zero). The probabilistic calculation is highly *uncertain*. There is, moreover, a continuum of possible situations (and hypothetical urns) between e_2 and e_3. One might suppose, for example, 342 samples from the U_2, or 36, or 8.

The notion of *weight* covers, in the same way, the distinction between *uncertain* and *improbable*. Keynes will refer to this in the *General Theory*. The sense of an event's *improbability* is linked to some kind of judgment about simple, or first-order, probability. The sense of *uncertainty* is linked to a second-order probability estimate (the event's *weight*). An estimate of weight is therefore a deeper, almost epistemological, look at the plausibility of the probability estimate. The two dimensions of *probability* and *weight* are both essential to understanding the probability of events, broadly construed.

The Uncertain and the Unknown

Let us summarize the preceding arguments. The notion of *weight*, for Keynes, is a *judgment of confidence* of statements about what is real; it is an evaluation of the reliability of information as obtained by experience. When the weight is zero or close to zero, the situation is one of uncertainty; people can give only a weak credence to their knowledge. What philosophical consequences about uncertainty may be drawn from this?

Uncertainty does not correspond (unlike improbability) to an "essential" characteristic of the world, as revealed by observing the mathematical frequency of an event. *Uncertainty* refers to a judgment about the *knowledge* of what is real or not. Put another way, it is a judgment on the *quality of available information about reality*. For Keynes, therefore, to push the reasoning, chance and determinism are not opposed concepts. The opposition is rather to be found between *chance* and *knowledge*. The only difference between chance and knowledge, as the philosopher and scientist Pierre Simon de Laplace observed, is ignorance (Laplace 1902).

In Keynes's own words, "The terms certain and probable describe the various degrees of rational belief about a proposition which different amounts of knowledge authorise us to entertain" (*CW* 8:176). Explicitly, uncertainty is brought back to lack of knowledge; the terms "certain and probable" are associated with "rational belief" as determined by available knowledge. It is, therefore, this expression, *rational belief*, that we shall now examine.

Keynes's Position on Logical Probability

Keynes's reflection on uncertainty led to a new concept of probabilistic theory. He developed new rules of calculation to apply to it.

Probability as an Expression of Weak Logic

Chance is, in Keynes's view, the absence of knowledge. Notions of what is probable may be viewed as a list of thoughts about a world that is deterministic at the same time that it is largely unknown. For Keynes, probability constitutes a kind of thinking mechanism of human logic that becomes connected to a weakened causal relationship. It implies a relationship between an ensemble of premises, h, and an ensemble of conclusions, a; the probability, p, represents the degree of rational belief that can be attached to this implied relationship. In other words, probability gives us the degree of confidence that can be given to a logical proposition. As Keynes wrote, "Between two sets of propositions, therefore, there exists a relation, in virtue of which, if we know the first, we can attach to the latter some degree of rational belief. This relation is the subject-matter of the logic of probability" (*CW* 8:6–7).

The mechanism p, therefore, specifies the causal relationship between two groups of propositions, h and a. The link between h and a is not perfect. The use of the value p (always less than 1) indicates that the link is *weakened; p* defines a probable causality between h and a.

In 1921 Keynes therefore adheres to a *logical* interpretation of probability with which he opposed the frequentist interpretation. More precisely, Keynes tries to reconcile the two positions through the use of his distinction between probability and weight. Simple probability is derived directly from observation. It may be considered an inductive step, as frequentists would believe. Weight, on the other hand, is more logical than inductive in content. Determining weight is linked to a cognitive, or reasoning, step, that is not inductive in nature. Keynes thus opens the way to a new approach to probabilistic reasoning. What are the practical consequences that Keynes draws from this?

Rules for Calculating Logical Probabilities

Keynes's interpretation of probability calls into question, at least with regard to weight, the axiomatic rules generally used to calculate prob-

Figure 3.3 **Logical Probabilities Area**

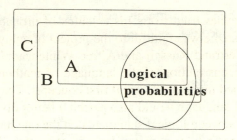

ability. Hicks (1979) illustrates the point with the following example. Assume three groups (Figure 3.3):

- A, which is a group of numeric probabilities. They are additive and comparable.
- B, which is a group of ordinal probabilities. They are comparable.
- C, which is a group of probabilities.

The logical probability of Keynes can belong to all three groups. But, outside of B, the classical rules of calculating probability no longer apply. Most notably, the axiom of comparability is abandoned. This means that with any two given propositions, either one is more probable than the other, less probable, or not at all comparable. In the case of noncomparability, the ordinal nature of probabilities ($P_1\ P_2$, or else $P_1 < P_2$), generally thought to be the basis of probability calculation, can no longer be verified. In the extreme, probability becomes immeasurable and cannot be represented by a real number between zero and one. Starting from these reflections, the hard core of the *Treatise on Probability*, its mathematical heart, is devoted to developing techniques for calculating logical probabilities. We shall not pursue this part of the work, which, to be frank, is hard going. More to the point is the methodological value of these ideas about probability.

The Relevance and Methodological Value of a Logical Position

This exposition of the main ideas in the *Treatise on Probability* allows us to discuss the intellectual parentage of Keynes's work to this point and, by extension, those whom he influenced.

Russell, Wittgenstein, Keynes

Very clearly, Keynes tried to tie his calculus of probability to formal logic. In doing so, he was faithful to the project of analytic philosophy developed by Bertrand Russell and Alfred Whitehead. Their goal was the complete reconstruction of the language of mathematics, starting with a very limited number of logical first concepts. The reconstruction of mathematical language would also permit a better division, in scientific discourse, between logical statements on the one hand and empirical statements or inductive statements on the other. Empirical and inductive statements were necessary to go beyond the tautologies inherent in an exclusively deductive discourse. This program also reflects the neopositivist ideas then exemplified by Wittgenstein.

The *Treatise on Probability* is therefore a lineal descendant of Russell and Whitehead's *Principia Mathematica* (1905). Keynes's study appears as an attempt to extend the field of formal logic to a larger domain, that of probabilities and weak causalities. And as a corollary, as we have already noted, Keynes wanted to demarcate the boundary between the inductive part, on probabilities of the first order, from the logical part, on probabilities ("weights") of the second order. It is entirely right to conclude, along with, for example, Favereau (1985), that the intellectual foundations of Keynes's thought are firmly anchored in the intellectual universe of early twentieth-century Cambridge.

Keynes, Ramsey, and Savage

Keynes did not just follow his brilliant mentors; he also started a new line of inquiry engendered by his own research. His thesis of logical probabilities, as mechanisms of knowledge, directly inspired a young Cambridge student, Frank P. Ramsey. Ramsey's work begins with a highly critical reading of Keynes's *Treatise on Probability*. Ramsey was destined to start a third current of probability theory; to the traditional frequentist position and Keynes's logical probability, he added the *subjectivist* approach. This position has since been developed by Bruno de Finetti (1937) and Leonard Savage (1954). In this view, *probability belongs to a perfectly subjective system of belief.*

Ramsey's view may be connected to an extreme version of Keynes's. Probability appears, here as well, as a mechanism of knowledge based on formal logic. This time, however, the use of induction of the first order is completely abandoned. Probability is henceforth subjective. It functions more to give meaning to human action than it does to reveal anything about the essential nature of reality.[3] Its justification, as a last resort, is turned toward action, so as to give it rational coherence. The use of probability stems therefore from a pragmatic initiative, as Keynes acknowledged in discussing Ramsey's thesis. For example, agents will use subjective probabilities to calculate the expected utility of their actions. Let us note that Keynes, in his review of the posthumous edition of Ramsey's article, agreed with this last subjective interpretation of probability. He pays homage to his friend and bows to his reasoning ("Ramsey as a Philosopher," *CW* 10:335–346).

Methodological Impact

We may well ask what Keynes himself found of use in his reflections on probability and uncertainty. How did his youthful research on these topics influence the future economist?

So far as economic decisions go, it is clear that Keynes's probabilistic reasoning will find its clearest expression in the realm of "expectations." Chapter 5 (on short-term expectations) and Chapter 12 (on long-term expectations) of the *General Theory* make reference to the *Treatise on Probability*. It is in writing about "the state of long-term expectation" (as Keynes titled Chapter 12) that Keynes expands his ideas about the behavior of economic agents in conditions of uncertainty. There can be no doubt that his previous work on the *Treatise on Probability,* especially on the noninductive character of some expectations (their weight), led Keynes to develop an original theory about their economic effects. Expectations, working in the absence of any credible factual basis, result from a self-referential logic that is reminiscent of the logical position developed in earlier years. We will return to this question when we discuss Chapter 12 of the *General Theory,* which also takes up the questions of mimicked expectations and shared conventions.

More abstractly, we might ask to what extent Keynes's early research on uncertainty penetrated into his deepest epistemological presuppositions. That is, it may have profoundly influenced how he conceived inquiry in the social sciences. Keynes's innovations on nonordinal and nonmeasurable logical probabilities may well explain, for example, why he decided not to formalize the *General Theory* into a mathematical model. Economic reality is not, in its entirety, measurable. It cannot be, so soon as one attaches a psychological dimension to it.

Moreover, Keynes's youthful work laid out a principle of weak causality that, *in situations of uncertainty,* provides a dark view of scientific reasoning. When *weights* are zero, the relationship between *h* (premises) and *a* (conclusions) does not exist. How, then, can one find such a relationship?[4]

Does this mean that all scientific undertakings are invalid in economics? Certainly not. Rather, Keynes insists that inquiry methodologies in the social sciences, especially tests of validity, must have particular forms. Most especially, he concludes that the economic sciences will not be able to construct universally valid truths. Lacking universality, economic science should at least be useful. Keynes therefore strives, as systematically as possible, to join his efforts, and that of economics in general, to a reasoned pragmatism. This, as we shall see, is characteristic of macroeconomics.

Keynes's methodological project was ambitious. It is strongly inductive, as can be seen from references to Russell's analytic philosophy. But it also uses, *at the highest possible level of abstraction,* the principles of formal logic.

Conclusion: A Simplified Equation

It is tempting to simplify the development of Keynes's thought to an equation: *Treatise on Money + Treatise on Probability = General Theory.* However, there is ample reason to think that this is not so. From 1930, when the *Treatise on Money* was published, until 1936, when the *General Theory* appeared, Keynes worked on a very different set of questions than those that had occupied him earlier. The unending economic crisis and the generalized appearance of mass unemployment, not just in Britain, but in many industrialized countries, changed many of the questions that concerned Keynes.

Nonetheless, the idea suggested by the equation, that the *General Theory* was to be built by taking the *nexus of monetary concerns* and adding it to an *inquiry on uncertainty in economics,* does give us a useful point of entry to a first reading of the great work of 1936. The *General Theory* presented the world with an audacious economic theory that started a new school of thought and a new paradigm. The *Treatise on Money,* on the other hand, is a prudent variation on some traditional themes; everything seems to show that in it Keynes did not break away into the world of heterodox thinking. This inhibition, which one does not often see in Keynes's thinking, no doubt helps to explain the failure of the *Treatise on Money*. It is, in some ways like the *General Theory,* a half-finished book. But whatever its deficiencies, the *General Theory* soars where the *Treatise on Money* merely plods. The seeds of the brilliance and innovation that characterized the mature scholar are more readily seen in the *Treatise on Probability* than in the *Treatise on Money*.

That is why, in fact, we reversed the order of presentation of these two works in this chapter. The *General Theory* is in no way a recasting of the *Treatise on Money* that preceded it. The work of 1936 is more ambitious. Because it sought to systematize the role of uncertainty in human life, the *General Theory* emerges, perhaps paradoxically, as closer in spirit and intellectual content to the earlier work of 1921. It is to the *Treatise on Probability* that the *General Theory* owes its revolutionary content and, in no small part, its success.

Notes

1. The simplification presented here has no government spending, no taxation, and assumes that the economy is closed to international trade.

2. We arrive at equation (5) by dividing both sides of equation (4) by Q. The right side of (4) becomes an expression of the price level, P.

3. Probability need not be founded a priori on an inductive process. Induction is reintroduced a posteriori following Bayes's rule, which provides the transformation principle of a probability when a new event occurs.

4. A question later pursued by Vercelli (1991).

4

The *General Theory* (1)

A Reader's Guide

The *General Theory* earned Keynes even more fame than his *Economic Consequences of the Peace*. It won him an intellectual following worthy of any of the greatest writers in the social sciences. The 1936 book established the framework for the debates and controversies of the last half of the twentieth century. It created a true school of thought around its central ideas. Members of this school found in the *General Theory* a vision of economic processes, a methodological concept, and a political platform.

Keynes's theses have, obviously, been widely debated. Still, the most striking aspect of these debates is that the most bitter controversies have not been between Keynes and the detractors of his thought, but rather between rival schools of interpretation. The *General Theory* is such a rich mix of ideas that even a single insight leads to multiple rival interpretations, each based on or another aspect of the text. There is no single key to reading the work, but many.

This fact considerably complicates our presentation. Because we are trying to present these often-conflicting interpretations in an introductory manner, we shall not attempt to endorse one over another. Some authors, most famously Joan Robinson (1962b), consider other authors' positions to be "bastard Keynesianism" and have inspired others to use that adjective even for their book and article titles (see, for example, Turgeon 1996 and Kregel 1983). In spite of these passionate disagreements, a complete account of the disputes over the major passages of the *General Theory* would bog down our presentation. The pages that follow cannot do full justice to a half-century of debate.

The presentation in this book follows a particular outline that attempts a reasonable, perhaps moderately bastardized, compromise between choosing a single interpretation and presenting many rival interpretations in depth.

This chapter presents the *General Theory*'s overall structure by following the construction of the book as Keynes wrote it. Even here, there is a risk of interpretive bias. Nonetheless, the chapter insists on two key conceptions in the work: the existence of distortions in the labor market and the role of uncertainty in economic relationships taken as a whole. We will especially focus on monetary relationships. The following chapters will analyze the basic mechanisms and then turn to the problem of competing interpretations.

The Labor Market: Point of Departure for Keynes's Causal Framework

Keynes begins the main exposition of his book in Chapter 2, titled "The Postulates of Classical Economics." This chapter focuses on how the labor market works. Keynes begins by outlining the main principles that underlay traditional economics. He tries to introduce a new idea about the labor market: its distortions are inevitable, so it is more fruitful to look elsewhere for ways to reduce unemployment. This is Keynes's point of departure. We will follow his arguments step by step.

The Postulates of the Classical Economics

Chapter 2 on "Postulates" follows a very brief Chapter 1 (only half a page long). Chapter 1 defines the term "General" in the title and states Keynes's objective: the integration of classical theory as a *particular case* in Keynes's own theory. Keynes explains what he means by "classical": *all* of past economic theory, lumping together the Ricardian and the marginalist schools.

Analysis as such begins in Chapter 2, where the postulates are defined, argued against, and the consequences of those arguments outlined.

The Classical Position

Keynes identifies two postulates that are central to the classical theory:

- P1: Real wages are equal to the marginal productivity of labor.
- P2: Real wages are equal to the marginal disutility of labor.

By wages, Keynes means real wages, and he says so explicitly. This is typical classical reasoning. Nominal values are automatically converted into sums that deflate any potential change in prices.

The postulate P1 reflects, from the point of view of businesses, a criterion of rational behavior in the choice of factors of production. The labor factor is used so long as its cost (wages) is less than or equal to the value it produces (the marginal productivity of labor). Only a few imperfections in the state of competition can, for a short time, work against this rule. The postulate P1, by precisely linking the total employment of labor to real wages, is in fact the *labor demand function*. For each potential wage rate, *w/p,* there is a level *N* of labor demanded by employers:

$$N^d = N^d\,(w/p).$$

This is a decreasing relationship: the higher wages are, the less profitable businesses will find it to employ workers. This rational principle for the determination of the demand for the labor factor stems from the desire of entrepreneurs to maximize their profits.

Postulate P2, in the classical tradition, describes the decisions made by workers. It says that workers offer their labor as a function of the prevailing wage rate. For very high wages, a large number of workers will be willing to work. At low prevailing wages, however, many will choose to withdraw from the labor market. This definition of behavior gives us the *supply function of labor.*

$$N^s = N^s\,(w/p)$$

In modern terms, this function could be described as a rational choice between work and leisure.

The simultaneous solution of these two postulates, as held by the classical theorists, determines the volume of employment. Figure 4.1 shows the intersection of the supply and demand for labor.

Figure 4.1 **Voluntary Unemployment**

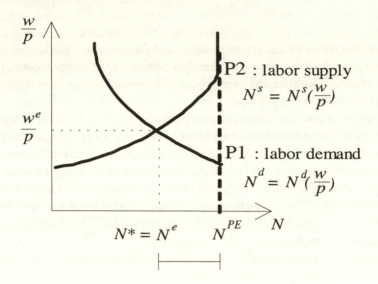

The theory that follows from this way of representing behavior can only explain unemployment as temporary or, especially, *voluntary.* Between the level of employment determined by the joint solution of the two postulates (N^e) and the level corresponding to the employment of the total active population (N^{PE}), a gap may open up. Nonetheless, because of postulate P2, it can only result from a deliberate decision to withhold labor by workers. The wage rate is simply not enough to make the workers *decide* to offer their services to employers. Graphically, the quantity ($N^{PE} - N^e$) indicates the number of "voluntarily unemployed" workers. (We will return later to the use of $N^* = N^e$ to indicate the volume of employment actually realized.)

This, then, is the theory of unemployment that Keynes attributes to the classical economists, in particular to Pigou (1933), who had just published his own *Theory of Unemployment.*

Keynes's Position: Involuntary Unemployment

Keynes argues against the classical position on unemployment. To him it is obvious that unemployment is not always *voluntary,* a point that he emphasizes even at the risk of oversimplifying Pigou. However, Keynes does accept the first postulate. He readily concedes that businesses follow a rational criterion in hiring workers. But he argues against the second postulate: withdrawal from the labor market is not always the result of a decision influenced by real wages. Keynes raises two objections to this notion. The first objection "is not theoretically fundamental." The second objection, on the other hand, *is* "fundamental" (*General Theory* 1964, 8).

The first objection concerns how workers *perceive* the level of their real wages. Workers cannot easily measure their wages against variations in price levels. They are subject to a monetary illusion: wrongly, they do not immediately perceive a rise in prices as equivalent to a lowering of their real wage. Logically, such an observation weakens the relationship in P2, without, however, refuting it over the long term. For, over the long term, agents will realize their mistake. It is, therefore, the second objection that is the most important.

The second objection to P2, and therefore to the entirety of the classical theory, is contained in the following words:

> The traditional theory maintains, in short, *that the wage bargains between the entrepreneurs and the workers determine the real wage . . .* [yet] the assumption that the general level of real wages depends on the money-wage bargains between the employers and the workers is obviously not true. (*CW* 7:11–12; italics in original.)

What Keynes objects to, then, is the assertion that negotiations over the nominal wage can set, at the same time, the real wage.

Before examining Keynes's reasons why there is no negotiation over the real wage, let us first note the consequences of falsifying postulate P2. The immediate result is the possible appearance of involuntary unemployment. The determination of the real wage outside the labor market presages the emergence of a *false price* for labor, that is, a price that will leave either employers or workers unsatisfied. More precisely, to the extent that P2 is shown to be wrong, it is the supply of labor that is going to be insufficient. This is graphed in Figure 4.2.

For the prevailing real wages, we can see that there is a gap between the demand for, and supply of, labor. The volume of labor effectively employed is proven to be set along the length of the postulate P1 : $N^* = N^d$. But, at this level of real wage, the supply of labor is greater. The

Figure 4.2 **Involuntary Unemployment**

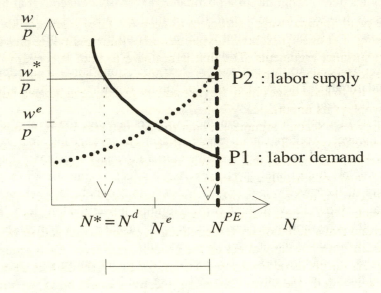

unsatisfied portion $N^s - N^*$ is a population of *genuine involuntarily employed workers*. That is, they want to work at the prevailing level of wages, but cannot find jobs.

In Walrasian terms, involuntary unemployment, to be even considered, must be integrated into a framework of rigid real wages, which show no flexibility. Rigid wages keep the labor market from clearing, that is, they guarantee that more people will be seeking jobs than there are jobs to be had. Up to this point, however, our reasoning has been partial; we see, in Figure 4.2, only the labor market and its failure to clear. From here we shall quickly pass to reasoning based on general equilibrium.

Rigidity of Nominal Wages, Real Wages, and Prices

Keynes has therefore established a *necessary condition* for abandoning the classical beliefs about employment and their conclusion about the voluntary nature of unemployment. An imperfection in the way real wages are negotiated means that, in practice, the supposed propensity of labor markets to clear has failed. We are still only a few pages into the *General Theory*. Now we must find the causes of the labor market's failure to clear and the ways to remedy it. Keynes leads us on step by step.

Nominal Wage Rigidity: A Necessary but Insufficient Condition

Are rigid nominal wages sufficient to keep the labor market from adjusting? Let us see first how Keynes describes this rigidity. He provides two succinct arguments. The first is not hard to find. It concerns the classical bogeyman, unions, which, to protect the interests of their members, try to keep wages high. Keynes admits that this can happen but he downplays its importance. We shall see why.

Keynes's second argument, about the *relative* real wage, is subtler. Agents are opposed to reductions in their nominal wages because they reject the justification that is given: reduce nominal salaries to reduce costs, and get a healthy deflation for everyone.

According to Keynes, workers think this theory of virtuous deflation is bunk. They expect that other wage earners will reject a wage reduction and that a deflationary wage reduction policy would neither be enforceable nor have any effect on the general price level. Each group of workers rejects its own wage reductions, because it thinks that all other workers will do the same. Cascading rejections would bring the whole price level containment process to a halt—or, more likely, it would not even start. Workers, therefore, behave rationally in avoiding any reduction in wages, so as not to be sucker-punched by everyone else. The nominal wage level is virtually nailed in place by this instinctive reaction to protect relative purchasing power.

This is the relative wage thesis, and it argues that wages and the general price level are inextricably bound together. Keynes uses it to develop a more plausible notion of wage rigidity. In fact, Keynes claims that focusing only on explanations of *nominal* wage rigidity is by itself insufficient. It is the rigidity of the real wage that needs to be explained, not the nominal wage. One could, indeed, easily imagine a shift in prices that allows the real wage to reach its equilibrium level. As a technical matter, there are two ways to make a fraction w/p coincide with a predetermined value $(w/p)^e$ that restores equilibrium: one is to shift the numerator, w, but as we have seen, wages are not easy to change; the other is to shift the denominator, p, the level of prices.

Keynes will show that this second technique also will not work.

Real-Wage Rigidity and Price Rigidity: A General Perspective

The rigidity of the nominal wage is an insurmountable obstacle to full employment only when it is accompanied by an inadequate setting of price levels. That is the message of the *relative wage thesis*. It is the necessary condition for real wages to have no possibility of reaching a level where the market for labor clears. This is the basic idea that Keynes will pursue. In his own words:

> There may exist no expedient by which labour as a whole can reduce its *real* wage to a given figure by making revised *money* bargains with the entrepreneurs. This will be our contention. We shall endeavour to show that primarily it is certain other forces that determine the general level of real wages. The attempt to elucidate this problem will be one of our main themes. (*CW* 7:13; italics in original)

The real wage, which could virtually assure equilibrium, is not negotiated. Keynes acknowledges that bargaining occurs over nominal, or money, wages, but he does not concede bargaining on the real wage. From the nominal to the real wage, there is only one intermediary: the *general price level*. In the Keynesian system, a simultaneous determination of prices overwhelms initial contracts on wages. To reconsider our mathematical analysis of the real wage, negotiating the numerator [the w in $(w/p)^e$] will not bring the labor market into full employment equilibrium if at the same time it is nullified by a shift in the denominator [the p in $(w/p)^e$]. All his life, Keynes opposed the idea (attributed by him to Pigou) that reducing nominal wages would solve the unemployment problem. In the terms presented in the second chapter of the *General Theory*, the only plausible explanation of this position lies in the unfavorable interaction between nominal wages and price levels.

So where does one find the determination of price levels that immediately undermines preliminary contracts on wages? Keynes must now face this problem.[1] Now, indeed, he must borrow from a general equilibrium perspective. Obviously, the general level of prices is not negotiated on the labor market. The level of prices is set by certain other factors that, in practice, will require the integration of another market, perhaps many other markets. In other words, he has to abandon the partial perspective of focusing only on the labor market.

Keynes thus turns to the principle of *effective demand*. This principle explicitly sets the general level of prices and employment as a function of the expected conditions of many interdependent markets.

Figure 4.3 **The Equivalence Postulate**

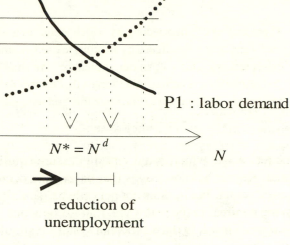

The Equivalence Postulate and the Causal Nexus

In Chapter 2 of the *General Theory*, nonetheless, before clarifying the concept more clearly, Keynes insists on what we now call the "equivalence postulate" (e.g., De Vroey 1997). The equivalence postulate posits a direct relationship between effective demand's determination of the employment level, on the one hand, and the determination of price levels, on the other.

To assert this strict equivalence, Keynes refers back to postulate 1 (referring to when prevailing wage levels are higher than the equilibrium level). Graphically, P1 (for prevailing wages higher than equilibrium level) establishes a one-to-one correspondence between the level of real wages and the level of employment.

The simple observation that *p* works in the denominator of the value of real wages, added to inspection of the graph in Figure 4.3, shows the *equivalence postulate* at work. Where nominal wages are rigid, every variation of *p* (every increase in price levels) is immediately accompanied by a modification (a decrease) in the real wage. Then, as Figure 4.3 indicates, along the labor demand curve P1, a variation (increase) in the level of employment follows. In Keynesian terms, this function may be

Figure 4.4 **Chain of Consequences**

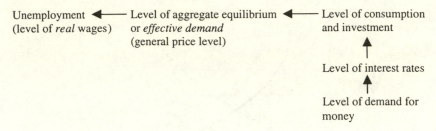

called an equivalence postulate between changes in effective demand and changes in the level of employment.

Already, then, by the end of Chapter 2, we can discern the general outline of Keynes's approach. (See Figure 4.4.) If you look at this diagram in reverse, following unemployment to the demand for money, you have, in fact, the structure of the presentation in Keynes's *General Theory*. The book is actually written as a chain of consequences, and each chapter takes us farther up to the origin of the problem with which we start. The book therefore has an organizational logic. It may briefly be summarized:

- Point of Departure: the falsehood of real wages (Chapter 2). Purpose: to determine how general price levels are established.
- Effective Demand (Chapters 3–7). Purpose: to analyze the forms of aggregate demand.
- Theory of Consumption (Chapters 8–10) and Investment (Chapters 11–12). Purpose: to analyze the forms of investment.
- Theory of Interest Rates (Chapters 13–14). Purpose: to analyze the forms of interest.
- Theory of the Demand for Money (Chapters 15–17).

We will end our analysis of Chapter 2 with two remarks. The causal diagram, as presented here, is extremely well known. However, many writers forget to specify that the first link of causality is price rigidity, the denominator that alters the determination of real wages.

We must point out that the presentation made at this point emphasizes the "neoclassical synthesis" version of Keynes's work. This school emphasizes fixed price levels as a key to reading Keynes. Our commentary on the second chapter of the *General Theory* necessarily leads to this type of interpretation. Even advocates of alternative readings, for example, Favereau (1985), see this chapter is a kind of patchwork. Perhaps Keynes intended this initial discussion of fixed prices to lure orthodox readers deeper into his book. So he baited his hook with ideas that were not too far from the dominant currents of the 1930s.

More radical interpretations downplay the importance of Chapter 2. Objections are made even to the idea of a labor market in Keynes. Our opinion is that this is a semantic problem. If we define a market as an abstract notion, as a theoretical meeting place where demand meets supply in *conditions necessarily regulated by flexible prices,* then there is no market. If we adopt a more flexible definition, usually accepted by economists, that the market is a place where supply meets demand under price conditions that may, eventually, be flexible, but which also may show rigidities, then, there is a labor market in Keynes. Even so, that observation does not mean that economic agents are the prisoners of the market. Because of the imperfections and flaws they find in the market, agents may actually use backup or alternative strategies. Market procedures and regulations may be used along with other coordination strategies that are better adapted to the unstable, uncertain environment in which agents know they live and make decisions.

Which leads us to our second remark. The causal nexus in Figure 4.4 in fact reflects the title of Keynes's work itself: *The General Theory of Employment, Interest, and Money.* Keynes evidently explicitly wanted, from the beginning of his book, to show the path he would take. It is a chain of logic. Almost everything is laid out, except, perhaps, the mainspring of all these mechanisms: uncertainty. And this is the second key to reading his book.

General Equilibrium: Uncertainty, Money, and the Interest Rate

As we have seen, Keynes presents the causal nexus of the *General Theory* in reverse order. There is, however, a unifying thread that runs through the entire argument. As we proceed up Keynes's causal ladder from an effect, to a cause, to a new effect, and a new cause, we see that there is one ever-present element: uncertainty. This idea, which Keynes had already studied in the *Treatise on Probability*, now becomes a systematic element of his argument. Uncertainty permeates Keynes's notions of economic behavior and causality; it is used to round out, and sometimes even as a substitute for, the more comfortable notion of market equilibrium. Uncertainty is, in a word, a general tool with which to interpret economic reality.

As many other scholars observed, the key arguments about uncertainty are perched in Chapter 12, midway through the *General Theory*. This chapter is devoted to the state of long-term expectations. It is of pivotal importance, coming immediately after the analysis of real economic output (pertaining to consumption and investment) and just before the chapters on monetary analysis as such (pertaining to the interest rate and liquidity preferences). Nonetheless, uncertainty makes its first appearance well before Chapter 12. In Chapter 3, for example, the introduction to the topic of effective demand puts the notion front and center. Arguably, the use of uncertainty in this chapter is more devastating for classical economic theory than anywhere else in the book. It is here that, logically, we are led to understand that the general level of economic activity, and hence the level of employment, result from the general state of expectations. We begin our exploration of uncertainty at this point.

Uncertainty and Decision Making by Entrepreneurs: The Principle of Effective Demand

We will first take a look at the principle of effective demand. We will then, as Keynes did, consider its implications, especially regarding its main theoretical competitor, known as Say's law.

Expected Demand and Effective Demand as a Principle

There are many competing ways to graph Keynes's basic idea. We have chosen, in Figure 4.5, one proposed by Weintraub (1960).

The *aggregate supply price, Z,* shows a relationship between the general level of employment set in motion by employers and the cost of production.

At every level of employment there corresponds a level of unit production costs for aggregate production. This is a positive relationship: the more economic activity there is, the more resources are used, and the more businesses have to pay for them. The convex curve, Z, in Figure 4.5 is not strictly necessary; the chief fact is that its slope must be superior to D's.

The *expected proceeds of employment, D,* correspond to the *possible*

Figure 4.5 **Effective Demand Principle**

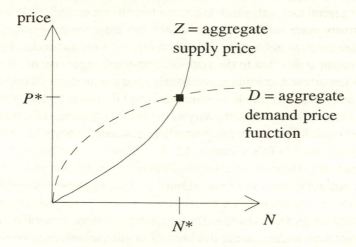

unit sales prices of production. Keynes also called *D* "*the aggregate demand function*" (*CW* 7:25). Demand also depends on the level of employment. When the level of employment is high, more income is distributed. Therefore, there are more potential buyers willing to pay for the aggregate production. Nonetheless, the form of the curve, *D,* is concave, because people's willingness to buy goes up as production does but by smaller and smaller increments as their income rises. On this last point, however, Keynes makes more of an affirmation than a proof. He works on this problem through much of the book, bringing in his own novel approaches to consumption and investment as part of his analysis of this point.

Let us now think about what these two curves mean. Keynes argues that aggregate equilibrium between the level of prices and the level of employment is fixed exactly at the intersection of these two curves. The point of intersection, *DE,* is the point of *effective demand*. To the left of *DE,* the prices of goods would be higher than costs. Businesses would make excess profits. Businesses would then try to increase production and would compete for resources. The level of employment would rise and move the economy back closer to *DE.* To the right of *DE,* businesses would lose money. They would cut back on their investment activity. This would also, on the graph, bring them back to point *DE.* In the end, employment and price levels must be exactly at the point *DE.* They cannot do otherwise.

The point of effective demand, which at the same time gives us the effective level of employment, therefore strictly determines the level of general equilibrium. To Keynes's way of thinking, the principle of effective demand is preferred to the notion that the job market determines employment levels. For the job market is inefficient, as has been seen. Nevertheless, the dual determination of prices (on the ordinate) allows us to see how the principle of effective demand affects real wages and induces disequilibrium on the labor market (via the denominator); in short, we verify the equivalence postulate discussed above. Let us turn now to what this principle means.

The Missing Auctioneer and the Asymmetry of Entrepreneurs

Expectations determine the equilibrium level of economic activity: such is the major message of the principle of effective demand. For as is clear, businesses set the level of employment in relation to their expectations regarding eventual purchases by consumers. Yet consumers' total purchases are a function of their income, and the total income of an economy depends on total employment. The level of economic activity set in motion thus depends entirely on how entrepreneurs estimate the future level of the incomes that they themselves, as a group, will pay.

Thus, a particular class of economic agents, the entrepreneurs, determines the equilibrium level depending on how optimistic or pessimistic their feelings are about the future. Moreover, this is a double determination. Entrepreneurs set both the total quantities of goods produced, *and their prices,* in the manner they see fit. This theory is altogether innovative. It abandons the traditional fiction of prices set by a market equilibrium between supply and demand.

Lacking a hypothetical Walrasian auctioneer to give them reliable information, entrepreneurs are on their own when it comes to deciding how much to produce and how much to charge. Here we find trace elements from debates on imperfect competition: businesses unilaterally set their prices, without regard to any supposed *general* market clearing imperative (in the Walrasian sense of general equilibrium).

Indeed, disequilibrium theory or non-Walrasian equilibrium theory, which we have already discussed (see pp. 63–66), has its origins in the principle of effective demand. One might see this particular interpretation of Keynes as illustrative of the new Keynesian economics, or NKE. Given rigid pricing strategies, disequilibriums bounce quantitatively from one market to another. The expectation of shortages in one market adversely affects the employment level and, through it, the level of distributed income. This very fact confirms the entrepreneurs' expectations of limited markets.

Matters do not end there. In this way of looking at the economy, at the heart of the system of economic relations, a powerful asymmetry is revealed. The entrepreneurial class has a perfectly dominant position: the expectations of this group alone construct an equilibrium out of a situation that was, a priori, in disequilibrium. Most especially, the entrepreneurs distribute the income that, in fact, validates the equilibrium they themselves have established.

In this respect, we should look again at the curves in Figure 4.5. They have a concrete, real value only at the single point, *DE*. Apart from the point *DE*, they remain only the graphic representation of expectation. Concerning the aggregate demand function (*D*), for example, entrepreneurs establish, for every level of employment *N*, a level of *notional demand*. The level of notional demand is based on entrepreneurs' collective expectations with regard to the behavior of consumers and of other investors. But this becomes *effective demand* only when the income that creates *DE* has been paid out. The principle of effective demand, therefore, is not just a description of the real economy (*DE*). It is a description of *what entrepreneurs think* about the economy.

It is fruitful to compare the economic theory that Keynes attributes to entrepreneurs with a rival, classical view first proposed in 1803 by French economist Jean-Baptiste Say (1767–1832).

Say's Law and Self-Fulfilling Expectations

The principle of effective demand is therefore a description of a mental process that leads entrepreneurs collectively to set the level of equilibrium. As early as Chapter 3, Keynes insists on comparing his principle with an established, competitive theory. Let us admit that entrepreneurs are not worried about the size of their markets. Or, perhaps, let us say that as faithful readers of the great classics of economic theory, entrepreneurs forge ahead, putting their faith in Say's law and its view of markets. What would be the result?

Say's law holds that a market *must exist* for products that are offered for sale. In other words, *supply creates its own demand*. As Say wrote in the *Treatise on Political Economy*: "The success of one branch

Figure 4.6 **Say's Law**

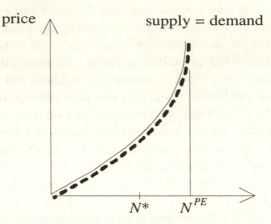

of commerce supplies more ample means of purchase, and consequently opens a market for all the other branches . . ." (1964, 135). The producer, when he pays for the factors that he uses in production, automatically creates a purchasing power that corresponds to the monetary value of his product. At the macro level, there must necessarily be equality between aggregate supply and aggregate demand. This is shown graphically in Figure 4.6.

This description of how equilibrium is determined naturally leads to the conclusion that it does so at a level of full employment. Since potential markets do not constitute a constraint on production, general equilibrium must, by default (and thanks to the competition between entrepreneurs), set itself at the full use of all factors, including labor.

By contrast, the principle of effective demand leaves open the possibility of equilibrium levels that do not provide full employment. Yet Say's law indicates there must be full employment. Which perspective is right? The answer is clear if one has fully understood the self-fulfilling, psychological aspect of Keynes's principle of effective demand. This principle describes, as already discussed, a mental process about economic mechanisms. But the mental states of entrepreneurs enjoy a dominant, privileged position: their expectations become reality.

As investors, entrepreneurs set in motion the funds that they think they prudently may spend. These funds become the income of those who work for them. So investors create exactly the aggregate purchasing power that will validate their expectations!

So which is true: Keynes's law of effective demand or Say's law? In a word, both may be true. Keeping Keynes's self-fulfilling principle of effective demand in mind, we see that Say's law becomes one possible outcome in the universe of Keynes's self-fulfilling prophecies. If investors firmly believe in Say's law, they will collectively spend and provide a level of income that leads to full employment, and Say's law will be true. But if they lose faith and fear a crisis brought on by insufficient demand, they will cut back on their level of investment and validate the very crisis that they feared. In other words, Say's law may be kept for the special condition of equilibrium itself. The principle of effective demand describes the expectations, themselves outside of the equilibrium state, which may (or may not) lead to full employment equilibrium.

The self-fulfilling prophecies of entrepreneurs are therefore the stuff out of which equilibrium is made. Their pessimism leads directly to depression, their optimism brings about an economic upturn. These self-fulfilling prophecies allow us to sort out, among the many different equilibrium levels possible in Say's law, the level of equilibrium that will be realized.

Such is the leitmotif in the *General Theory:* economic reality depends on general beliefs about it. These beliefs about reality, in their turn, determine which of many possible outcomes becomes real. Expectations about reality create reality. More precisely stated, it is the *convergence* of expectations around a common norm, a *convention,* that in the end determines equilibrium: a single pessimistic entrepreneur cannot by himself or herself make a recession. Indeed, he or she would be seriously amiss in expecting such a thing while his or her peers charged ahead without sharing his or her view. But when pessimism itself becomes the norm, then recession becomes inevitable. It matters little whether there is any "real" basis to the pessimistic reasoning: the only thing that counts is what other business leaders believe.

The owner of a firm asks: Are others expecting a recession? Will they stop paying out the income that their employees need to buy my own products? This kind of questioning inevitably leads to thinking about what others believe still others believe. Entrepreneurs collectively may sink into a depressive norm, but their beliefs also may lead to an economic "pact for growth."

The process of estimating economic reality, and its validation, is not just self-fulfilling; it is *self-referential,* or, as some systems analysts like to say now, *recursive*. Everyone looks around to see what others are doing. Business owners are driven to imitate each other.

Entrepreneurs are, in fact, rational in imitating one another. That is exactly how one discovers where the norm is and, therefore, how one correctly solves the problem of adhering to it. Indeed, a volume edited by Orléan (1992) and a separate work by Dupuy (1992) focus precisely on the *mimetic rationality* found in Keynes. The self-referential quality of entrepreneurs' decisions is all the more crucial in that they are plaintiff, judge, and jury: they distribute the income. It is they who directly decide an important part of aggregate demand: investment. Investment is, as we shall see, the most dynamic element in determining economic activity, but it is also subject to the widest range of fluctuation.

This interpretation of the principle of effective demand is essential. Uncertainty and expectations save economics from Say's law; without them, we are left in a predictable world where outcomes are determined in conformity with accounting principles. Uncertainty is therefore at the heart of the process of determining general equilibrium: such is our, and Keynes's, credo. Nonetheless, we must add that the these reflections about uncertainty and the self-referential nature of economic activity do not come early in Keynes's book; only in Chapter 12 will he lay them out more fully. In Chapter 3, which focuses on effective demand, Keynes merely inquires as to what objective reasons could simultaneously explain entrepreneurial pessimism, weakness in effective demand, and deviations from Say's law. In this respect, money's role is going to be extremely important.

Uncertainty, the Interest Rate, and Money: The Liquidity Principle

Aggregate demand determines the general equilibrium, objectively and subjectively, as we have just seen. Now we need to know why it is set at one level rather than another. Aggregate demand may be broken into two parts: consumption and investment. A fundamental psychological law determines consumption; we will come back to this law later. Here it suffices that, for our purposes, the essential dynamism of the economy lies not in consumption, but in investment. Variations in effective demand occur primarily because of changes in investment.

Investment, in its turn, depends on the interest rate. High interest rates tend to discourage investment. As Keynes himself noted in a BBC radio interview in 1931, the interest rate is the villain of the play. Indeed, the interest rate is the hinge between the monetary economy and the real economy in Keynes's causal nexus. An excessive interest rate is the cause of a crisis. Keynes's originality in this subject is linked to the monetary dimension he attributes to the interest rate. To understand his thinking, we must, here as elsewhere, look at the role of uncertainty. In this case, we are now concerned with its role in the demand for money.

Uncertainty and Money: The Speculative Motive

Uncertainty is present in the very premises of monetary relations. Keynes gives three basic reasons for holding money, of which one is directly related to uncertainty. Let us review Keynes's analysis.

Keynes's three reasons for holding money are the transaction motive, the precautionary motive, and the speculative motive. The transaction motive is in fact the classical argument for holding money: monetary balances are used to cover transactions. The precautionary motive stems from the desire of agents to hold a fixed sum against sudden and unexpected expenses. Put colloquially, the precautionary motive relates to "rainy day" funds that people put aside against the unforeseen.

The transaction and precautionary motives do not challenge classical theory because they have no real consequences on the proportional relationship (k or $1/v$) established between the aggregate level of economic activity and money balances. It is only the speculative motive that, by contrast, leads to a different conclusion. We shall consider its concrete forms.

The speculative motive establishes a new relationship between money deposits and interest rates. To understand this relationship, we must consider two levels of behavior. One level concerns the individual choices of an economic agent; the other level considers the aggregate behaviors of many individuals.

Individual behavior. At the individual level, an agent must decide how to divide his or her financial wealth between two principal categories: the purchase of securities, or holding his or her wealth as money. The interest rate regulates this relationship.

More precisely, the agent who wants to do a good job of managing his or her wealth must try to foresee future changes in interest rates:

- An increase in the current interest rate causes investors to prefer lending at the new rate. The price of older bonds (loans) in financial markets falls (causing their own real interest rate to rise). If the interest rate is destined to rise, it is advisable not to hold wealth in long-term bonds.
- On the other hand, a decrease in the interest rate causes bonds issued earlier, at a higher rate of interest, to increase in value. If interest rates are destined to fall, it is advisable to hold as much wealth as possible in long-term bonds.

The demand for holding wealth in the form of money will now vary according to speculative needs. An investor fearing a major rise in interest rates will try to stay *liquid*. That is, he or she will try to keep his or her wealth in the form of money or near-equivalents (such as short-term loans known in the United States as the "money market" or "commercial paper"). By doing so, he or she avoids the decline in value that will affect long-term bonds and also will be positioned to take advantage of the better rates once they occur.

At the individual level, therefore, the expectation of variations in future interest rates plays a role in determining people's preferences for holding money.

Aggregate behavior. People's expectations are a function of their fears; the *threshold level* is the point at which people reverse their preferences for holding money or longer-term securities. Investors are diverse, heterogeneous individuals, but as a group, they exhibit a collective behavior. This brings us to the second level of our analysis. Imagine, as shown in Figure 4.7, that we arrange investors as a function of their *levels of fear,* or risk aversion. The most risk-averse people are assigned a value of 1 and the least risk-averse a value of 5.

A low rate of interest (on the ordinal) yields a unanimous opinion from investors. Since interest rates are very low, they cannot go much lower; they can only go up. Investors understand this and decide to avoid potential losses in the long-term bond market by staying in cash. The demand for money, at a low interest rate, is therefore at its highest. All the groups on the abscissa, from the least risk-averse (group 5) to the most risk-averse (group 1), together want to have "short," or "cash" positions.

Nonetheless, as the interest rate rises, we will see that the least risk-averse investors, and then the next risk-averse, will gradually decide to purchase longer-term securities.[2] As shown in Figure 4.7, the interest

Figure 4.7 **Money Demand**

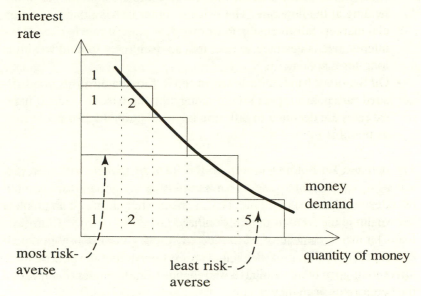

rate eventually reaches a level at which only the most risk-averse investors still wish to hold cash instead of making longer-term investments.

The demand for money and the interest rate may therefore be summarized as follows. At high rates of interest, only the most risk-averse investors will want to "stay liquid," or keep their money in the form of cash. At very low rates of interest, almost everyone will prefer to hold cash, or, as Keynes wrote, "to hoard." There is therefore a continuous, inverse relationship between the demand for money and the interest rate.

Liquidity and Specific Interest Rates: A General Theory
for Holding Durable Wealth

Economic agents' desire to hold money is therefore linked, in essence, to uncertainty. To Keynes's way of thinking, we could even go so far as to say that uncertainty is crystallized in money to the point that the two are, as ideas, interchangeable. Money especially concerns us because of its *liquidity*. An asset's liquidity is the possibility, ease, and speed with which investors may shift their wealth to another asset. They do this to protect themselves from the unforeseen events that might affect the real value of their goods. This is why money is so linked to uncertainty: it is the most liquid "good" of all, and it is the tool investors turn to when they are afraid. *Liquidity preference* is the concrete form through which individuals' fears are manifested.

Liquidity preference, as a principle, has been more generally examined as a "theory on the holding of durable commodities" in Keynes's *General Theory* (*CW* 7:222). In Chapter 17, Keynes furnishes a justification for the endeavor by distinguishing "three attributes which different types of assets possess in different degrees" (*CW* 7:225). These may be paraphrased:

- A physical asset's yield or output q. This is estimated as a percentage. For a capital good, q corresponds to the good's value output (its marginal *productivity*). For a consumption good, q corresponds to the good's direct marginal *utility*.
- The maintenance cost, c, needed to keep an asset in usable condition. This cost, c, may be stated as a proportion of the good's value and thought of as a capital maintenance cost. It applies to almost all assets except money.
- A liquidity premium, l, that is directly linked to uncertainty. This represents the sum that agents are prepared to pay (expressed as a percentage of the good they are holding) to be sure of being able to unload this durable asset on someone else, immediately and without constraint.

Having defined the three terms q, c, and l, Keynes makes a new proposition. Every good may be thought of as having an "own interest rate." This is the rate of interest each good would earn if interest payments were made in more of that good. Thus interest on wheat would be paid in additional wheat. The own interest rate of each good or type of wealth may be written:

$$\text{own interest rate} = q - c + l.$$

Every type of asset may therefore be evaluated by its own interest rate. Or, put another way, it may be evaluated with regard to *the expected service it will provide its owner.* Keynes wants here to *correct* the traditional way of thinking about asset q's return by adding two variables. Adding c is mere common sense. Adding l is especially important because it emphasizes the profound uncertainty that governs economies. Certain kinds of assets are highly liquid. They command a high liquidity premium, *l,* because holding these assets protects, or at least is supposed to protect, their owners from uncertainty. On the other hand, certain goods are highly illiquid. People who hold these assets face significant losses in the event of an unfavorable turn in the economy. The liquidity premium of these assets is therefore very low.

Here Keynes has resolved an enigma of economic theory. Why is money, whose profitability, in and of itself, is zero, so often preferred to assets that are more productive and even more profitable? The answer, following Keynes's formula, is immediate: money's limited direct profitability (low value of q) is compensated by its extremely high value from the point of view of liquidity (high value of l). Money may, therefore, be rationally preferred to a more profitable asset.

Keynes goes on to specify that agents are constantly using their judgments about specific interest rates on specific assets in order to choose among different potential investments. Theoretically, all these specific interest rates will fall to a common level. When the specific rate of return on a good is higher than average, it will attract investment, up to the point that the rate of return on that good begins to fall. The decreasing marginal utility of each new investment in that good leads to decreasing marginal returns for investors. So, in equilibrium, the interest rate of money is necessarily equal to the other specific interest rates on various assets.

The decreasing marginal return of each new investment leads us to a closely allied concept: what Keynes called the *marginal efficiency of capital,* or MEC, and its relationship to the interest rate. The MEC is the interest rate on specific capital: its estimated return, corrected for maintenance costs and a (usually small) liquidity premium. The specific rate of interest on money, however, is the *standard interest rate,* the rate at which money is borrowed. Business management must choose when to hold money as cash and when to make real investments in production. Rationally, business managers choose to invest up to the point where the marginal efficiency of capital equals the standard interest rate. The interest rate therefore functions as a floor for the MEC. This is shown graphically in Figure 4.8.

Technically, as we see in Figure 4.8, the money rate of interest (on the ordinal, or y-coordinate) forms an incompressible threshold for the MEC. On the abscissa, or x-coordinate, this threshold has a direct effect on investment choices in the real world. Weakness in investment is therefore a direct outcome of uncertainty among holders of capital, of an excessive rate of interest, and of the liquidity preference that corresponds to it. What, indeed, could be more risky than to invest in productive

Figure 4.8 **Marginal Efficiency of Capital (MEC) and Investment**

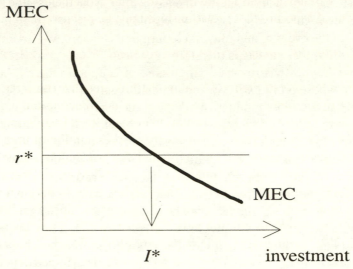

capital, by its nature fixed, when the markets for goods are uncertain?

So businesses are fundamentally affected by uncertainty when they make choices between "cash positions," or liquidity, and investment. (At this point Keynes clarifies his ideas by introducing what he calls the *finance motive*, which we will examine at greater length in the remaining chapters of this book.) Business managers' choice of finance (using retained earnings versus contracting debt) reflects their liquidity preference. Their liquidity preference, a barometer of their optimism or pessimism, indicates their psychological well-being. When businesses are less willing to go into debt (to use bank credit), they are showing a relative preference for liquidity, or holding more of their own cash. A high liquidity preference means they have fears about developments in the broader economy. High business debt levels, on the other hand, are usually a signal of business optimism. Though it is tempting to believe otherwise, high debt levels are not always indications of poor financial health among businesses.

Reviewing the Causal Nexus: Uncertainty, Hydraulic Thinking, and How to Represent Something by Its Opposite

The fundamental cause of underinvestment is uncertainty and the preference for liquidity. This is Keynes's basic message. We can summarize this reasoning in three graphs, as in Figure 4.9. These three graphs show how the different causalities are linked together. Nonetheless, the purely mechanical aspect of these relationships must be discussed.

The "Hydraulic Summary" of Keynes's Causal Nexus

The three graphs of Figure 4.9 show the linkages that run from equilibrium in the money market to general, or macroeconomic, equilibrium. This is a textbook representation derived from Paul Samuelson. For now, this is preferable to yet another representation of core ideas in the *General Theory*, the IS-LM model that we shall examine later. Figure 4.9 offers some advantages over the IS-LM model because it reproduces the sense of causality that Keynes gave to his own work, which runs from the money market (figuratively, "upstream") to the level of employment (figuratively, "downstream"). The "upstream" graph, 4.9c, on the right, shows the equilibrium reached between a given demand for money (at some previously determined level) and the quantity of money in circulation (the money supply). This money supply is assumed to be exogenous, determined by the monetary authority. The center graph, 4.9b, has already been discussed (pp. 121–122). "Downstream," however, graph 4.9a represents an entirely new situation that must be explained.

The line at $45°$ ($Y^d = Y^s$) is a simplified quantitative expression of the principle of effective demand, which, as we know, determines the overall level of economic activity. Here, however, we have passed from thinking about the *prices* of the supply of goods to thinking about the *quantities* produced and demanded. We have lost something of the refinement of Keynes's analysis, for he was also interested in general price levels. Nonetheless, we preserve a central element of this thinking: goods become available only to the extent that, in the minds of entrepreneurs, a market for them exists. Graphically, this hypothesis is shown along the bisecting $45°$ line, which shows all the points that mark the equilibrium levels where total supply, Y^s, is equal to the entrepreneurs' estimate of total demand, Y^d.

Nonetheless, demand itself remains to be calculated. Aggregate demand consists of two major components: investment and consumption. The "upstream graphs" (4.9b and 4.9c) illustrate how investment is determined. We have, up to this point in our discussion, treated consumption as the "poor relative" of Keynes's family of ideas. However, in

124

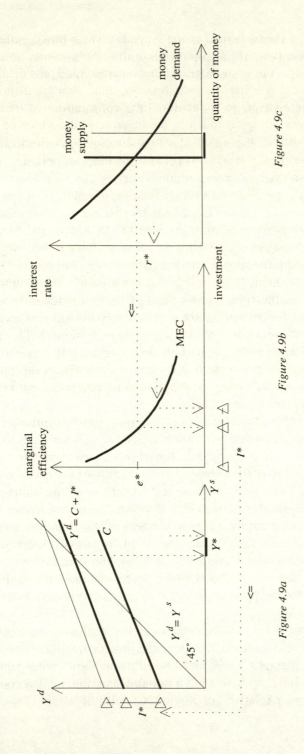

Figure 4.9 **Keynes's Causal Nexus: Hydraulic Summary**

Figure 4.9a

Figure 4.9b

Figure 4.9c

Chapter 8 of the *General Theory,* Keynes gives a broad outline of the consumption function in macroeconomics. He presents an argument based on both "our knowledge of human nature" and "the detailed facts of experience." We may be sure, he says, that "men are disposed, as a rule and on the average, to increase their consumption as their income increases, but not by as much as the increase in their income" (*CW* 7: 96). This is, in Keynes's words, "a fundamental psychological law" that may be expressed mathematically as follows:

$$C = f(Y), \text{ where } 0 < (\delta C/\delta Y) < 1.$$

Stated informally, whenever personal income goes up, personal spending goes up also, but not as much as income. Stated formally, the marginal propensity to consume (the mathematical derivation of consumption in relation to income) is positive, but less than unity. The richer societies become, the more they consume, but the *share of income* that is devoted to spending tends to get smaller as income gets bigger. The tendency of growth in spending not to match growth in income helps justify Keynes's attention to investment as the key to economic performance: because the propensity to consume is diminishing in relation to total income, economic dynamism must be found elsewhere in the economy.

To restate, we may consider the following linear function as a way to represent Keynes's consumption function:

$$C = cY + C_o \text{ where } 0 < c < 1, \text{ and } C_o > 0.$$

This consumption function corresponds to the line *C* drawn in Figure 4.9a. The connections between Figures 4.9a, 4.9b, and 4.9c should now be clear. They provide a simplified but cogent way to study the interactions of some of the principal themes developed by Keynes. We might, for example, consider the following variation. Imagine that the money in circulation is increased (in 4.9c, the heavy black vertical line shifts to the right, shown by a thinner line). Almost mechanically, the following things happen: the monetary stimulus lowers the rate of interest (as shown by the new level *r** in Figure 4.9c). The lower rate of interest (moving now to Figure 4.9b) increases the marginal efficiency of capital and stimulates investment (a shift to the right on the lower axis of Figure 4.9b). The increase in investment raises aggregate demand over its previous level (we are now in Figure 4.9a; the heavy black line, $Y^d = C + I^*$, is increased to the level of the thin black line above and parallel to it). This stimulates an increase in aggregate supply (a movement shown on the line $Y^d = Y^s$). The result is a boost to output (a movement to the right of the heavy black bar Y^* on the lower axis, Y^s) and therefore of employment.

Alex Coddington (1976) baptized this simple chain of reasoning the "hydraulic model" of interpreting Keynesian theory.

Between the Cup and the Lip: Uncertainty and the Inadequacies of the Hydraulic Model

However, Keynes himself warned against a simple mechanical interpretation of his causal nexus. In his words:

> We have now introduced money into our causal nexus for the first time, and we are able to catch a first glimpse of the way in which changes in the quantity of money work their way into the economic system. If, however, we are tempted to assert that money is the drink that stimulates the system to activity, we must remind ourselves that there may be several slips between the cup and the lip. (*General Theory* 1964, 173)

The famous slips to which Keynes refers may be summarized in a few words: they are linked to the extreme instability of human behavior under conditions of uncertainty. Nonetheless, let us be clear that uncertainty does not play an exclusively destructive role in the hydraulic causal chain presented by Samuelson. Rather, the construction of these causal chains depends completely on the fact of uncertainty; in its absence, the causal chains would not exist. For example, uncertainty about developments in financial markets is an essential element of the demand for money, the speculative motive that we discussed earlier. Indeed, uncertainty is a necessary condition for the very fact of having an interest rate that is affected by the quantity of money (as in Figure 4.9c).

Nonetheless, even though uncertainty is integral to reasoning about the economic system, it establishes only weak causal relationships.

First, we have to recall that all of these relationships are based on expectations. Expectations about changes in the rates of interest determine the demand for money in Figure 4.9c. Expectations about the profitability of capital (marginal efficiency of capital) are key to Figure 4.9b.

Expectations about effective demand govern output in Figure 4.9a. The stability of the curves, how they are placed in the various graphs, depends on the main hypothesis: that agents have a stable degree of confidence with regard to economic developments.

Then, we may review how various kinds of uncertainty impinge on the hydraulic schema:

> *Figure 4.9c:* The monetary stimulus that, we have said, should lower interest rates could be neutralized in advance. This would happen if an increase in general anxieties about changes in interest rates caused people to hold more money (speculative motive). This pushes the demand for money up and negates the increased money supply's potential to stimulate the economy above its previous level of output.

> *Figure 4.9b:* If the expectations of entrepreneurs about the future profits of capital are declining, their estimate of the marginal efficiency of capital will lower the MEC curve. This change in their expectations could negate the stimulus of lower interest rates.

> *Figure 4.9a:* Entrepreneurs' estimates of effective demand always have a psychological element. Figure 4.9a does not show this well, because the 45° line implies that supply is somehow always set to meet demand. Nonetheless, assuming that a monetary stimulus has successfully been transmitted from Figure 4.9c to Figure 4.9b, in Figure 4.9a the possibility remains that entrepreneurs may have a very dim view of the future demand for their goods. So, even here, for the monetary impulse to work, there must be a *collective state of anticipation* among business investors that translates into an *effective increase in income.*

> *Figure 4.9c (again).* When all is said and done, and an increase in aggregate income has indeed occurred, there may still be a negative effect back at the beginning of the chain. The transaction demand for money increases, attenuating the impact of the initial monetary stimulus. (This effect, called the monetary brake, is more easily discussed with the IS-LM model, to which we will return.)

The effect of a monetary stimulus depends heavily, therefore, on a series of hypotheses about the psychological disposition of agents. This leads us to two reflections. First, we may better understand Keynes's preference for direct action on the volume of investment, rather than indirect action on monetary policy. Public works policies and socialization of investment do not need the series of favorable conditions required for the successful use of monetary policy, which attempts to influence private investment through the interest rate. Public works and state investments have an *immediate* effect, in the proper sense of the term.

Moreover, our remarks on the underlying assumption of stable expectations in Figures 4.9a, 4.9b, and 4.9c also point to the extremely fragile nature of a successful economic policy. When agents are generally optimistic with regard to economic policy, the level of confidence rises. The curves move favorably (the speculative demand for money decreases, the MEC increases), and the hydraulic model of monetary policy, aided by the cooperation of economic agents, appears to work well.

On the other hand, if investors do not like economic policy, there is such generalized anguish that liquid or "cash positions" are preferred to every other investment. In this case, a monetary stimulus will only confirm investor's pessimism and give them new money to stick into their bank accounts.[3] The demand for money and the interest rate will remain high, as an index of the general level of anxiety, while all hope of an economic revival languishes.

In other words, the success of a Keynesian economic recovery program depends, above all, on the massive support of the public it is intended to help.

Here we see again the self-fulfilling, self-referential, or recursive qualities of economic expectations. If agents believe in Keynesian policies, those policies will work; if collectively they do not believe in them, those policies may fail. In Chapter 12 of the *General Theory* Keynes develops his ideas most fully, describing the general behavior of agents faced with uncertainty. In the end, everything depends on the conventional beliefs that agents establish with regard to economic conditions. Pessimistic conventional beliefs lead to a general preference for liquidity. The interest rate stays high in spite of hydraulic efforts to lower it. Optimistic conventional beliefs, on the other hand, work to verify the main assumptions of the hydraulic model.

Arrous (1982, 858) sums up this position rather well:

> As a general rule, the long-term state of expectation stays the same, because of conformity to optimistic conventional beliefs. The hydraulic approach derives its justification from this optimistic convention. In the

conditions thus postulated by this approach, we can reason about aggregates that are stable by assumption. We can carry out a mechanical, fully deterministic analysis of the economic system. But, the state of expectations, which govern investment, are based on extremely volatile data. . . thus investment, even viewed at the macro level, remains capricious and unstable. In fact, so soon as doubt is introduced, the difficulties linked to uncertainty become irrepressible. The impossibility of a mathematical calculus that can serve as a guide to rational behavior makes the elimination of doubt even more problematic.

Conclusion: A Call to Action

We have briefly reviewed the *General Theory*. The causal nexus is summed up in Figures 4.9a, 4.9b, and 4.9c. Nonetheless, these three graphs also contain the principle of uncertainty that undermines their mechanistic or hydraulic linkages. This paradox demonstrates the complexity of Keynes's work, even its contradictions. The *General Theory*, indeed, may lead us to multiple interpretations, all more or less valid depending on our goals or the perspectives from which we read.

Nonetheless, two major themes have emerged from our reading. The first concerns the possibility of distortions on the labor market and the need to adopt a general equilibrium approach rather than a partial equilibrium approach to the problem of unemployment. The second concerns the role of uncertainty, which disturbs economic relationships and leads us to attribute a special function to money, based on its liquidity.

Still, beyond the disputes of specialists, we need to come back to Keynes's basic message. The common denominator of all his thoughts, all would agree, is that unemployment does not have to be accepted as a fatalistic necessity. Keynes's ambition, and therefore the principal aim of the *General Theory,* is to construct an analytical framework for the specific needs of *economic policy.* Keynes's macroeconomics led immediately to important extensions of his thinking. These developments require a careful examination, which is the subject of the next chapter.

Notes

1. When we reach this part of the argument, we are at page fifteen of the *General Theory* (*CW* 7). Keynes will devote the next 300 pages to its analysis.
2. "Securities" is a general term that refers to both bonds and stocks. Investors

who buy stocks today are making a judgment about the value of future dividends from those stocks. The "dividend" of a bond is its interest payment or "coupon," and investors look at these payments in much the same way that they look at the payments from high-dividend stocks.

3. Such liquidity preference appears to have hampered economic recovery in Japan in the 1990s, in spite of "Keynesian stimulus packages" that in a purely hydraulic Keynesian world ought to have increased aggregate demand. The interest rate cuts of 2001–2002 in the United States also generated weak investor response, in contradiction to the pure hydraulic model.

5

The *General Theory* (2)

Macroeconomics

The most important test of Keynesian theory is, no doubt, its ability to provide ways to reduce unemployment. Macroeconomics, as a guide to economic policy, is therefore the most immediate practical extension of the ideas in the *General Theory*. Here we must show how Keynesian theory can be used to intervene effectively in the economic cycle and its consequence, unemployment.

As for economic cycles, the interest rate appears as the central variable in many theories. Authors such as Wicksell, Hayek, and Dennis H. Robertson had, before Keynes, already pointed the finger at the interest rate as the central issue. All three of these theorists served as Keynes's precursors and two of them, somewhat later, as his critics. Keynes nonetheless brought new life to the debate on the interest rate because he turned away from variations in the rate of interest as such. Rather, he subordinated considerations about the savings-adjustment process to a different mechanism: the multiplier, which led to the view that investment must precede savings. In the pages that follow, different interpretations of the multiplier will be analyzed, because they influence our understanding of the *General Theory*.

The Interest Rate as the Core Analytic Problem of Economics

Keynes's analysis of the economy at the national level launched a new discipline within economics. Today, we call it macroeconomics. Nonetheless, Keynes's efforts were not new. Before him, Knut Wicksell (1851–

1926), Friedrich von Hayek (1899–1993), and Dennis H. Robertson (1890–1963) analyzed fluctuations in economic performance and the relationship of these fluctuations to the interest rate. In this section, we will briefly review the ideas of these authors. Here we are not attempting, as in the discussions of Marshall and Walras in Chapter 2, to provide an objective summary of these authors' work. Rather, we will focus on Wicksell and Hayek, only to the extent that their thought mirrors Keynes's own developing ideas.

Knut Wicksell

Wicksell's *Lectures on Political Economy* (1901–1906) are often described as a work full of useful intuitions. From these intuitions Keynes supposedly gathered part of his ideas for the *General Theory*. Certainly, the two had shared interests on a number of points. Nonetheless, the answers they provided were different. Wicksell was a classical economist who remained fundamentally opposed to the idea that money had a long-term effect on the real level of economic activity.

Wicksell's Economic Cycle: A Summary

Our summary of Wicksell's ideas on cycles will use contemporary economic tools: a graph and a few simple equations. Wicksell proposes that economic cycles may be explained by maladjustment between the *monetary*, or the *effective rate of interest*, and what he called the *natural interest rate*. This maladjustment has the particular quality of making itself worse over time.

As in Figure 5.1, the spread between the two rates of interest takes the form of disequilibrium in financial markets.

When the real effective interest rate r_1 is set so that it is lower than its equilibrium level (the natural rate, r_n), a relatively high level of investment follows. Banks make credit available at relatively low cost and entrepreneurs borrow heavily. The growth phase of the cycle has begun. At the same time, investment spurs additional demand for goods (labor factors, natural resources, machines, and so on). This has an effect on prices: inflation begins to appear because of excess aggregate demand. At this point, the higher price levels are going to have an additional effect. The natural rate of interest r falls even further (r_1 to r_2 in Figure 5.1). This is because $r \approx i - p$, where p is the inflation rate and I is the nominal interest

Figure 5.1 **Wicksell's Model of Economic Cycles**

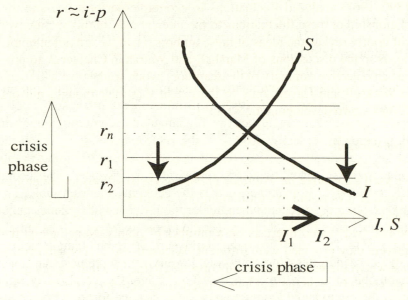

rate; as prices rise the real rate of interest falls, based on the assumption that i remains constant. The spiral continues because the new level r_2 leads to another increase in credit and then to more inflation. And so the cycle continues, increasing the investment-savings disequilibrium.

However, Wicksell foresees an end to the process of increasing lending and decreasing real interest rates. He argues that household savings will become scarce and with them the funds needed to finance investment. Credit institutions are caught in the contradictory pull of increasing demand for loans and decreasing deposits from the public. The stability of the banking system becomes increasingly precarious. The banks are headed toward a dangerous threshold at which their reliable sources of funds are insufficient to meet the many lending needs. The banks respond by raising their nominal interest rate, i, in order to attract new deposits and discourage new borrowing. The U-turn arrows in Figure 5.1 depict this reversal in the movement of the interest rate.

The change in the nominal interest rate causes r to move toward the natural rate r_n. In fact, r may even overshoot r_n. When this happens, interest rates are artificially high. The investment cycle is interrupted, and if it reverses itself, the economy enters into a crisis.

Wicksell's Economic Cycle: Some Analysis

Wicksell's cycle is very similar to the economic cycle Keynes described in the *Treatise on Money*, as has been remarked. We would like to add a few additional thoughts.

For Wicksell, the growth phase of the economic cycle may be extended. The effects are cumulative: inflation, far from leading to an immediate correction of the disequilibrium, makes it worse. Today's economic theory distinguishes two fundamental and contrary effects in an inflationary economy. The first, the *real balance effect,* is, on the whole, a stabilizing force. Faced with increasing prices, economic agents reduce excess demand by adding to their deposit balances. The second effect, *the flight from money,* makes the economy more unstable. The flight from money occurs when, under the influence of anxieties about the future value of the currency, people prefer to get rid of it as rapidly as possible. They draw down their bank deposits to buy things (modern experience indicates people buy gold, jewelry, other currencies, and even automobiles) that will more or less hold value. People also buy right away simply to avoid having to pay a higher price for the same goods later. All this panic buying, or flight from money into goods, adds to aggregate demand. As a result, inflation picks up speed.

In fact, in his theory of the economic cycle, Wicksell describes something akin to the flight from money. This, too, is a cumulative cycle. Wicksell differs from the standard theory by applying it to the investment behavior of businesses.

Wicksell's theories are often described as the first intuitions of *disequilibrium theory*. Prices, including the rate of interest, are *false.* For example, the effective interest rate is false, because it differs from the "natural," equilibrium interest rate. There is no Walrasian auctioneer to tell banks the correct interest rate, information that they need a priori to bring capital markets into equilibrium. The maladjustment between the effective interest rate and the natural interest rate is in fact what causes economic cycles.

What is more, Wicksell takes into account the interactive effects between different markets. His viewpoint is systemic and Walrasian, even though Figure 5.1, which shows only one market, might make us think otherwise. Therefore, the disequilibrium in the broad markets for goods and services has an impact, through price inflation, on the real interest rate. This has an impact on capital markets, and the initial disequilibrium is, as a result, made worse.

In spite of these insights, however, Wicksell is no Keynes. Wicksell's focus on money and the interest rate at no time causes him to question the classical theory. Most especially, the inevitable cyclical return to equilibrium in the banking sector and changes in the nominal interest rate show that Wicksell adheres to the long-term *neutrality* of monetary effects. Wicksell is closer to the Keynes of the *Treatise on Money* than he is to the Keynes of the *General Theory*.

Friedrich von Hayek

Hayek's influence on Keynes's development parallels Wicksell's. The questions Hayek asks are similar to Keynes's, but his answers are fundamentally different. Hayek's work is, moreover, contemporary to Keynes's: he became known in Cambridge in the early 1930s and gave a lecture in England on his book, *Prices and Production* (1931), the same year that it was published. Keynes took some pleasure in arguing with Hayek, whom he esteemed as an intellectual sparring partner. Hayek nonetheless directly opposed Keynes's ideas, and his *Prices and Production* appeared at a crucial moment between Keynes's *Treatise on Money* and the *General Theory*.

The Austrian Capital Theory and the Concertina Effect

Hayek was born in Austria and educated in Vienna. He built on theses advanced by the Austrian school, especially the work of Eugen von Böhm-Bawerk (1851–1914) and Carl Menger (1841–1921). (See, for example, Böhm-Bawerk 1959, and Menger 1950.) Capital is viewed as a production detour, a process also called "roundaboutness." A farmer could plant corn in the ground by digging holes with his hands. If he takes time to craft a hoe, he will be able to plant more efficiently. Constructing the hoe is a "detour" in the process of planting corn, a "roundabout" but ultimately more efficient way of getting to the task.

More formally, roundaboutness is known as the average period of production. The formation of capital (machines, tools, buildings) corresponds to a detour in the allocation of primary resources. These resources are channeled away from consumption goods toward sectors that produce capital goods. This is done to accumulate capital goods so that, in the future, it will be possible to consume more with less effort.

The more numerous the production detours, the more productive the economy. Primary resources are transformed into industrial products (coal and iron ore became steel). Products like steel are turned into machines (such as production lines). Finally, the production lines are able to use energy (such as from coal) to shape raw materials (such as steel) into complex consumable goods (such as automobiles). The number of "production detours" varies from economy to economy; some might have three, others ten.

Investment beyond simple replacement needs is seen as creating a new detour. This is how Hayek came up with the *concertina effect*. (The concertina is a type of accordion). The productive structure of an economy may be thought of as a pyramid. Each layer of the pyramid corresponds to the number of production detours. One starts with the primary resources at the very top and works down toward the consumption goods.

Let us imagine, as Hayek did, that after a monetary stimulus by the public authority, the interest rate falls. As with Wicksell, business profit margins rise. Businesses respond by investing more. As they do so, a new production detour is added to the economy. The pyramid becomes elongated, as shown in the middle of the three pyramids of Figure 5.2.

As we can see, the base of pyramid II is necessarily narrower after it has been elongated by an additional production detour. Hayek sees a rivalry between the consumption and capital sectors for productive resources. The total area of the pyramid remains constant because the total use of production factors is assumed to remain constant. Therefore, allocating more to an upstream sector decreases the resources available to the downstream sectors. In other words, in the short term, a new production detour reduces the total goods available for consumption. This is the Catch-22 of the concertina effect.

Is the reduction in available consumption goods acceptable to consumers? A priori, not at all.[1] Productive activities and employment levels are still at the same level. Total income and therefore the demand for consumption goods has not changed. Unless there is some kind of miraculous intervention that makes people willing to defer consumption, there must result a condition of excess demand (or insufficient supply) on the market of consumption goods. The tension between supply and excess demand leads to price increases in the consumption sector. These increases rapidly affect the cost of production factors, especially through wages: wage earners want to maintain their purchasing power. Investors must therefore reconsider how much profit they can make in light of changes in wages. The

Figure 5.2 **Hayek's Concertina**

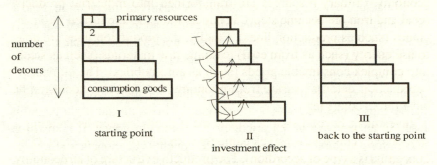

upstream businesses, at the top of the pyramid, see that the relative price of their production is declining, in comparison to the price of consumption goods and salaries. They conclude that the new production detour is not profitable. Investment ceases, and the pyramid contracts. The different stages of the pyramid all pass through the contraction crisis and, in the end, we return to pyramid III of Figure 5.2, which is exactly where we started.

The Concertina Effect: Some Analysis

Kaldor (1942) dubbed Hayek's stretching and contracting pyramids the "concertina effect," a not altogether respectful name that stuck. At a minimum, however, Hayek offers an original analysis of the macroeconomic cycle, and it merits a number of comments.

First of all, Hayek is proposing that a monetary stimulus has an effect on real output. In the short term, the upswing of the cycle, monetary interventions distort the productive structure. They create a *real,* and new, production detour in the economy, a new level in the production pyramid. It follows that in the contraction phase the effects are also real: the crisis affects all the different phases of the production process. Factories are closed: production capital gets cast aside. All these adjustments take time. The return to the starting point is long and costly, most of all in human terms.

The conclusion is clear: monetary interventions must be avoided at all costs. They obscure crucial signals in the economy (especially the interest rate) and create costly disturbances in the productive structure.

More fundamentally, Hayek offers us a theory of macroeconomic cycles that are linked to a lack of coordination between two decisions: savings and investment. Usually the interest rate is assigned the role of coordinator. Maladjusted interest rates, caused by government intervention, send a bad signal: invest. The investment decision is neither accepted nor validated by society. Household savings have not changed, which is to say that households have refused to accept the creation of a new production detour by forgoing the immediate consumption of some good. The investment decisions made by businesses are in the aggregate incompatible with the savings decisions made by households. This is disequilibrium, and it leads to an increase in the prices of consumption goods. It is also the reason for economic crisis and the ineffectiveness of monetary stimulus.

Keynes, as we know, did not share this view. Keynes's innovation, which seriously challenged the classical reasoning of Hayek and his followers, lay in his views of the adjustment process between savings and investment.

Prior Savings versus Post-Savings

In their conception of the economic cycle, both Wicksell and Hayek share at least one common vision. This vision is characteristic of classical economics and goes back to Ricardo, if not earlier. It can be described in two words: prior savings. It is this age-old concept that Keynes will challenge.

Prior Savings: Principles and Arguments

The principle of prior savings may be summed up thus: the total sum of all savings is given *before* the determination of general equilibrium. It is determined by the willingness of agents to save, and variations in the investment level are constantly butting against this sum. For Hayek, excess investment over savings provokes inflation. It leads to a crisis caused by a symmetrical shortage of consumption goods, as just discussed. For Wicksell, the same mechanism may be found buried in the bankers' books, where scarcity of deposits in relation to the credits allocated forces an adjustment of the interest rate. Nonetheless, in both cases the economic cycle turns downward because the social allocation of loanable funds has been exhausted. Savers cannot be forced to save more. Dennis H. Robertson (1953–1954, 138) likens the situation to the cliché about leading a horse to water but not being able to make it drink.

Keynes argues against the prior savings position. He bases his argument on what is now the well-known multiplier effect. Or, to alter Robertson's metaphor, the horse gets thirsty *because* it drinks. Devel-

Figure 5.3 *S* **Movement**

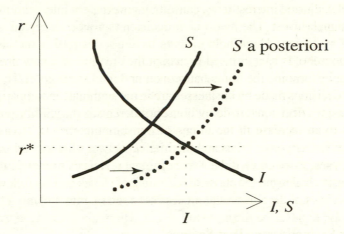

oped by Kahn in 1931, the multiplier effect shows the limits of thinking in terms of prior savings. In fact, Kahn describes the mechanism that leads savings to adjust *afterward,* to the level of investment that *precedes* savings. Investment therefore comes first, savings second, which we can denote by calling this alternative interpretation of the savings process "post-savings." This reverses the causality of the two variables, investment (I) and savings (S). S no longer leads to $I;$ rather, I leads to S. Figure 5.3 helps us visualize this idea, though almost every presentation of it is somewhat controversial. In Figure 5.3, the multiplier describes the movement of the S function, until it coincides perfectly with the level of investment. Compared to Figure 5.1 (Wicksell), a large increase in investment is now possible.

The reason for this movement is the increase in income. As soon as we cease to operate under the assumption that all production factors are being totally put to use, variations in the level of real income are possible. These variations, considering the way markets interact, prevent us from reasoning ceteris paribus. The curve S must shift the same time as the curve I.

Semantic Questions: Equality or Identity of I-S*?*
Toward a Spending Economy

With this definition of post-savings, as opposed to the more traditional prior savings, we are, as readers of Keynes, touching upon one of the most delicate points of exegesis in the *General Theory.* We have chosen these terms in an effort to achieve some theoretical neutrality. We therefore prefer *prior savings* and *post-savings* to the terms *ex-ante* and *ex-post*, introduced by Myrdal in a Stockholm lecture series (1931) and later published (1939). Ex-ante refers to *planned* investment and consumption levels and ex-post to *realized* consumption and investment levels.

The terms we use, *prior* and *post,* are not without fault. They imply a dimension of time that is sometimes considered arbitrary. They also imply that we can consider the creation of aggregate income only in a succession of discontinuous instants of time, T, between which nothing happens, except perhaps for the psychological reactions of people trying to anticipate the equilibrium level.

The most radical readings of Keynes argue against using a time dimension to describe the adjustment of savings-investment. In this view, the two macroeconomic categories are necessarily equal ($I = S$) or even identical ($I \equiv S$). This comes from both terms being defined as the excess of revenue over consumption. Therefore it is not necessary to refer to any kind of before-after process to describe their adjustment. They do not adjust because they are always the same, by definition.

In practice, the arguments are about whether the savings-investment adjustment can even be discussed in terms of market relationships and market equilibriums. The very notions of supply and demand of loanable funds, used by classical economists, are invalid to the extent that, in Keynes, saving *always* equals investment. To convince ourselves, we need only look at the equality, or perhaps even identity, of the way resources are available and used in the financial system (banks and other credit institutions). Arguing from this point of view, in Figure 5.3 (which we mentioned was controversial) the S curve would not move to coincide with investment, it would in all points be exactly the same as the I curve.

What may we say to this? How do we get past the equality versus identity debate? The simplest way is to focus on what the debate settles, rather than on the debate itself. The debate itself hinges on a semantic question that by its nature is insoluble. So what does the debate settle? We refer back to Keynes's original project. Armed with his new concept of the I-S adjustment process, Keynes showed that it is investment, by itself, that determines macroeconomic equilibrium, and it does so independently of all prior availability of resources (savings). Poulon (1985, 1987), putting the matter particularly well, characterizes investment as the boss of economic activity, not the underling; saving, as the underling, is subordinate and must always follow. So the *I-S* adjustment debate settles this: investment occupies the first and foundational place in the determination of aggregate income. This idea opens the door to an entirely new conception of economics.

Thus defined, economic equilibrium is freed, almost completely, from the constraints of scarce resources. In the classical spirit, this scarcity was thought to limit the equilibrium level of output. The interest rate remains as principal obstacle to the expansion of investment. Nonetheless, in Keynes's mind, the level of economic activity is no longer a prisoner of exogenous natural resource endowments such as land, minerals, or manpower that must be optimally allocated to secure the prosperity of the community. Henceforth, aggregate income is something that may be *built,* determined as it is by the entirely human decision to invest.

To paraphrase Alain Parguez (1987), we pass from the economics of scarcity, where predetermined allotments of resources must be divided up between competing uses, to the economics of spending. In the economics of spending, humanity invents and builds its resources. Human decisions are substituted for natural laws, sweeping aside the paralysis and fatalism that such laws inspire. Investment is an act that spurns the past and present, turning toward the future to *create* available resources. In doing so, it also creates the savings that now are a secondary consideration.

Is this to say that scarcity, as a principle of economic regulation, has been totally purged from Keynesian economics? Has Keynes so completely abandoned the categories of thought defended by traditional economists? The *General Theory* indicates that Keynes is not quite that radical, a term that we will reconsider in the next chapter. In many places, scarcity is reintroduced in his thought: always, it is attached to the interest rate. A consideration of the different versions of the multiplier effect helps us to understand this point.

The Savings-Investment Adjustment Process: The Simple Multiplier Effect and Its Extensions

A more detailed description of the multiplier effect is now necessary. It will help us understand some of the most basic principles of Keynesian macroeconomics. The notion of a posteriori savings shows a highly original concept of money and credit.

The multiplier effect, with its extensions and alterations, is basic to all economic analyses since the time of Keynes. Today's macroeconomics is built around core Keynesian notions put forward in the *General Theory,* regardless of whether economists accept or reject these notions. The IS-LM model, in particular, for better or for worse, has been particularly influential. In it, investment (*I*) and saving (*S*) are analytically linked as a single function (*IS*). The demand for money (*L*) and the supply of money (*M*) are also linked (*LM*). The two pairs, *IS-LM,* are one of the most widely used models in macroeconomics. But our purpose here is not to duplicate a course in macroeconomics. We are, instead, trying to see more clearly how Keynes established the relationship between prices, the interest rate, and unemployment.

Post-Savings and the Simple Multiplier Effect

The multiplier effect is above all a response of aggregate savings to a sum of investment. The sum itself is considered exterior, or exogenous, to the model. In its simplest version, which seems to be supported in the *General Theory*, the multiplier effect illuminates Keynes's position with regard to credit and money.

The Simple Multiplier Effect: How It Works

For practical reasons we will use in this section a few difference equations. The relationships among variables are not expressed for their absolute value (*X*), but in their variation (ΔX). The value of the multiplier proceeds from the two equations, which are solved simultaneously.

1. The first equation is the equilibrium of savings-investment, which comes from the equilibrium of jobs and resources on the market of goods and services. Entrepreneurs anticipate this equilibrium, following the principle of effective demand (refer back to Figure 4.9a on p. 124). The entrepreneurs, acting on their beliefs, set in motion the equilibrium. The following equation expresses the principle of income equilibrium:

$$Y^s = Y^d$$

The income stream above may be broken down. Y^s on the left is the savings and consumption of agents, Y^d on the right is the investment and consumption of businesses. These may be seen as:

$$S + C = I + C, \text{ or } S = I.$$

where S is saving, C consumption, and I investment.

Therefore, in the differential form, $\Delta S = \Delta I.$ \hfill (1)

2. The consumption function must now be differentiated. The marginal propensity to consume, c, appears:

$$C = f(Y).$$

In the differential, $\Delta C = c \cdot \Delta Y$

We also know that savings are the leftover of income less consumption. Therefore, $\Delta S = \Delta Y - \Delta C$. So, replacing ΔC with $c \cdot \Delta Y$, we get:

$$\Delta S = (1 - c) \Delta Y \hfill (2)$$

Using the simplified equations (1) and (2) gives the value of the multiplier. We get:

$$\Delta Y = \frac{1}{1 - c} \Delta I.$$

This determination of the multiplier, though mathematically correct, hides part of the economic intuition. It does not take into account the success of small variations that describe the multiplier as a process of adjustment to an initial investment. In Figure 5.4 we have graphed the process that leads savings to equal investment.

For an initial investment stimulus ΔI_0, and a consumption function $C = c \cdot Y + C_0$, we get:

$$\Delta_{total} S = (1 - c) \cdot [1 + c + c^2 + c^3 \ldots + c^n] \Delta I_0 = (1 - c) \frac{1}{1 - c} \Delta I_0 = \Delta I_0$$

Let us comment on the arrows in Figure 5.4. The initial investment ΔI_0 causes, as a direct effect, an increase in the equilibrium level of income by the same amount. The income having thus increased, consumption goes up too, in a proportion $c \, \Delta I_0$. This is shown as the first diagonal arrow. The increase in consumption causes, in turn, an increase in effective demand of the new sum: $c \cdot \Delta I_0$, which is the first horizontal arrow. This causes consumption to increase again in the proportion

Figure 5.4 **Dynamics of the Simple Multiplyer Effect**

	Effects on C	Effects on Y	Effects on S
Direct effect		ΔI_0	
First indirect effect	$\Delta_1 C = c\,\Delta I_0$	$c\,\Delta I_0$	$\Delta_1 S = (1-c)\Delta I_0$
Second indirect effect	$\Delta_2 C = c \cdot c\,\Delta I_0$	$c \cdot c\,\Delta I_0 = c^2 \Delta I_0$	$\Delta_2 S = (1-c)c\,\Delta I_0$
Third indirect effect	$\Delta_3 C = c \cdot c^2\,\Delta I_0$	$c \cdot c^2\,\Delta I_0 = c^3 \Delta I_0$	$\Delta_3 S = (1-c)c^2\,\Delta I_0$
. . .			
n^{th} indirect effect	$\Delta_n C = c \cdot c^{n-1}\,\Delta I_0$	$c \cdot c^{n-1}\,\Delta I_0 = c^n \Delta I_0$	$\Delta_n S = (1-c)c^{n-1}\,\Delta I_0$
. . .			
Sum of the effects $(n \to \infty)$		$[1+c+c^2+c^3 ... +c^n +...]\Delta I_0$ $= \dfrac{1}{1-c}\Delta I_0$	$\Delta_{\text{total}}S$ $= (1-c) \cdot$ $[1+c+c^2+...+c^n +...]\Delta I_0$

$c \cdot c \cdot \Delta I_0$, more easily written as $c^2 \cdot \Delta I_0$. This is the second diagonal arrow. The effect continues, approaching infinity. When we calculate the sum of the increases on Y, we find the value of the multiplier as previously determined.

During these different steps, the successive increases in distributed income logically lead (via the propensity to save, $1 - c$) to increases in the total level of savings. The column on the right in Figure 5.4 (Effects on S) shows these increases, which are summed at the bottom of the column. It is precisely in this number, the total savings, that we see the principle of the multiplier effect at work: we prove that total effect on savings comes back exactly to the value of the initial stimulus to investment. So $\Delta S_0 = \Delta I_0$. The story of the multiplier, when broken down, shows how the effect corresponds precisely to the succession of catch-up increases in savings, till the new equilibrium level of investment is reached.

The multiplier effect is therefore a process of "balancing" savings up to the level set by investment. The process continues so long as savings are inferior to investment. The causal chain of a posteriori savings stops only when the two have reached equality.

Nonetheless, as we observed in the preceding discussion of "equality versus identity," the temporal dimension implied in this description of the process may be taken with a grain of salt. The balancing of *I-S*, according to Keynes, is an integral part of effective demand. It is therefore really an *instantaneous mental process.* In other words, outside of the real point of effective demand, graphed in Figure 4.5 in the previous chapter, the succession of different phases is, to use the modern expression, "virtual," not real. The virtual adjustments are already integrated into the anticipations of entrepreneurs, who put to work the necessary sum such that $I = S$ and $Y^s = Y^d$. The "balancing" is immediate, instantaneous.

In this conclusion, the *General Theory* differs from the *Treatise on Money.* The concept of excess profit used in the *Treatise on Money* as an intermediate phase to account for an imbalance between *investment* and *saving* is no longer needed. Ordinary profits and excess profits are completely subsumed into income. At the point *DE* (see Figure 4.5) we can imagine points outside the real equilibrium. That is to say, we can imagine a situation in which expected costs and expected prices of goods to be produced differ. But in reality they must adjust so that they are always the same.

The deep cause of changes in the equilibrium is changes in the mental states of entrepreneurs that affect aggregate income. Here we come back to the Walrasian logic of interdependence among markets: the dynamic of equilibrium adjustment in one market (where *investment* and *saving* meet) is tied to other values theoretically set in other markets. We find again, as well, the idea of a fixed price equilibrium: the interest rate, which in classical economics adjusts *I-S*, plays a negligible role in the adjustment process. It is another market, or more precisely, *the labor market,* that adjusts the variables in responding to the expectations of entrepreneurs.

So, at this point in our analysis, we may note that the multiplier effect describes the economy as a bottomless well. Investment yields a proportionate level of demand in response, and, by implication, a proportionate level of saving. Here too, we find elements of the "spending economy," entirely determined by human beings and freed from the constraints of nature. Keynes even refers, in the *Treatise on Money,* to the parable of the widow's cruse, a jar of oil that never emptied (1 Kings

17:12–16). In Keynes's words, "profits, as a source of capital increment for entrepreneurs, are a widow's cruse which remains undepleted however much of them may be devoted to riotous living" (*Treatise on Money, CW* 5:125).

Should we therefore conclude that there are no restrictions to the multiplier and that we can therefore achieve unlimited economic activity? In the *Treatise on Money,* a limit is automatically imposed by the assumption of full use of the factors of production. In the *General Theory,* this assumption is dropped, but other limitations are taken into account, as we shall see later.

An Underlying Assumption: The Lack of a Liquidity Constraint. Bank Credit to the Rescue of the Simple Multiplier Effect

The multiplier effect, as here presented, may appear somewhat simplistic. Indeed, this is the form in which it is usually introduced in beginning macroeconomic classes. However, this way of presenting the multiplier effect has an underlying assumption: the independently generated investment stimulus is not halted by a scarcity of credit. In other words, as business investors first anticipate and then, by that fact, create an increase in income, insufficient financial resources cannot thwart their plans. This may appear to be a simplifying assumption. We may deepen the initial reasoning in adding a monetary component: the IS-LM model, which demonstrates the potential existence of a *monetary brake.* Through the interest rate, the monetary brake reduces the power of the multiplier effect to stimulate the economy.

The basic model gains subtlety if we relax the simplifying assumptions. In general, the so-called reductionist sciences must proceed in this manner: they give increasingly convincing explanations of reality as they abandon the strong versions of their initial hypotheses, which are considered too unrealistic. We will relax our assumptions later on; right now, we must first outline what the simplifying assumptions are. Our historical approach to the topic also requires us to ask: what led Keynes to formulate, and then accept the seemingly simplistic view of a multiplier without limits?

The idea of a simple multiplier requires a conception of money as a simple fluid whose level systematically adjusts to variations in investment and income. That is, the money supply adjusts perfectly to the needs of businesses. This easy adaptation of the money stock leads us logically to consider *money-creating processes*. There is one central arena for the convergence of monetary creation and investment: bank credit. Credit systems make money available exactly at the same time as investment decisions are made. Commercial banks literally increase the numbers in the account balances of their customers, the businesses that take out money as loans. This bank credit functions as a scrip money—used in transactions in the form of paper checks or electronic fund transfers. This bank credit, a kind of financial scrip, circulates as money among agents in the economy and is "good as gold" so long as the financial stability of the issuing bank is not in doubt. So when bank credit is issued to finance an investment, there is a simultaneous creation of real wealth (the physical investment) and the means to pay for it (the bank's credit, or financial scrip).

The objective limit of such a system of monetary creation is not at all clear. Monetary creation is validated through the accounting procedures of all banks. A withdrawal in one part of the banking system leads to a symmetrical, offsetting deposit somewhere else. In a phrase: Loans create deposits.

The limit to this process, if there is one, is grounded in banking practice: that is to say, it is institutional. The limit consists of a "reasonable" (or legal) ratio between banks' lending and their assets on deposit with the central bank. For every bank, directly or indirectly, has an account with the central bank. By limiting its own lending and its own monetary creation, the central bank is *theoretically* able to control the total credit available in the economy, which is to say, the stock of money.

Does the central bank freely choose how much money it will create, or is it forced to accommodate the demands of the economy? By lending at the "discount window," the central bank helps commercial banks satisfy shortages of funds. The central bank's choices here are highly constrained. Only rarely will the central bank allow a major public bank to suffer from a serious shortage of funds. Central banks are afraid that failures of major banks will lead to a general crisis of confidence that may threaten the entire banking system. In a *credit economy,* in which the central bank is obliged to furnish funds as the banking system demands them, the supply of money is *endogenous.* That is to say, the money supply is not determined by people following abstract principles or by forces "outside" the economy. Quite to the contrary, the money supply follows the level of economic activity: its growth accompanies lending needs, which follow variations in investment, which, in turn, follow effective demand.

The theoretical prospect of insufficient liquidity (money) is therefore eliminated by the relationship between banks, businesses, and the nature of credit itself. Banks and businesses are in a position to create not just real wealth, but the means of payment that will allow that wealth to circulate (a discussion may be found in Tobin 1963). Entrepreneurs enjoy a tremendous asymmetric position in this credit-based system: their hopes and fears determine their own demand for credit, the banking system's accommodation of that demand, and the economic activity that results. Everything depends on the entrepreneurial state of mind, which leads us back to the themes we have seen earlier: how uncertainty and the prevailing level of confidence cause businesses to sacrifice liquidity in order to assume the debt that will allow them to invest.

This analysis of credit and monetary creation underscores the perfectly subjective, self-fulfilling nature of Keynesian equilibrium.

IS-LM *with Fixed and Flexible Prices*

We have just seen how the multiplier in its simplest form fits with the theory of endogenous money creation. Now we must consider the contrary view, that of exogenous money.

Sir John R. Hicks (1904–1989) developed much of the reasoning behind the IS-LM model as part of a commentary on the *General Theory*. However, his "SI-LL" model (1937) did not achieve the now canonical title of "IS-LM" until the contributions (1949, 1953) of Alvin H. Hansen (1887–1975). Fastidious writers sometimes call *IS-LM* the "Hicks-Hansen" model. The IS-LM model clarifies the relationship of money to the multiplier in the framework of fixed prices. It adroitly takes into account the interactions between money and equilibrium. We will look at this model and then consider how flexible prices may then be introduced.

The IS-LM Model: How It Is Built, How It Works

$$Y = C(Y) + I(r) + G, \text{ with } \Delta C = c\Delta Y, \Delta I = I' \Delta r, I' < 0.$$

Here we find anew the principle, already discussed, of the balance between income and spending in the markets of goods and services ($Y^d = Y^s$). In addition to the equation showing equilibrium, income (Y) can be broken down into its component elements: *C, I, G* (consumption, investment, government spending). The sensitivity of private investment to the interest rate reflects the arbitrage process, or choices, that businesses make between liquidity and physical capital. This in turn is determined by the marginal efficiency of capital (as discussed in Chapter 4 and graphed in Figure 4.8). High interest rates reflect a crisis of confidence in the investment community. Investment is therefore weak when high interest rates prevail (yielding $I' < 0$). We introduce the variable G, government spending, to indicate the effects of a public policy of interventionism.

We now add a monetary component to the model of goods and services. The equilibrium equation for the supply of money, M, and the demand for money, L, or more simply, for the money market, LM, defines the following relationships:

$$M^s = M^d = L(Y, r), \text{ with: } L'_Y > 0, L'_r < 0$$

On the right, the demand for money is specified according to Keynes's ideas: it is an increasing function of income (the desire to hold money for transaction motives) and a decreasing function of the interest rate (the desire to hold money for speculative motives).

The differentiation of the two equations gives the following system:

$$\Delta Y (1 - c) = I' \Delta r + \Delta G \tag{IS'}$$

$$L'_Y \Delta Y = \Delta M^s - L'_r \Delta r \tag{LM'}$$

The first equation (IS') allows us to evaluate the direction of changes in income as a function of the interest rate. At the same time, the equation reflects the equilibrium in the market of goods and services: if $1 - c$ is positive, and I' is negative, the direction of change must be negative. In economic terms, an increase in the interest rate must have a dampening effect on the market for goods and services. An increase in the interest rate depresses investment, then finally (through the multiplier) depresses effective demand as a whole. This is why the I-S relationship is shown as a decreasing function when graphed on a plane with income (Y) and the interest rate (r) as its axes.

The second equation (LM') *also* allows us to evaluate the direction of changes in income as a function of the interest rate. This equation, however, also reflects the equilibrium in the money market: if L'_Y is positive, and $- L'_r$ is positive, the direction of change must be positive. In eco-

Figure 5.5 *IS-LM*

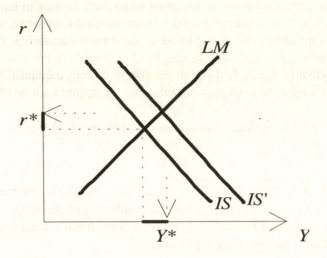

nomic terms: an increase in the interest rate dampens the speculative demand for money and leaves more money available to satisfy the transaction motive. (Remember, in this view, the money supply is exogenous, which means it does not increase or decrease in availability according to the levels of economic activity.) So, *all other things being equal,* income will increase. When graphed on a plane with axes (Y) and (r), the *LM* relationship is shown as an increasing function.

If we were to stick with this important qualifier, *all other things being equal,* we would have only a partial perspective. It seems to say, "let us think about what is happening in the money market and forget about everything else." The IS-LM model, and the Keynesian view more generally, insist, however, on the interaction of the different markets. The means to observe this interaction is to observe the interdependent equilibrium between the market for goods and services and the money market. The simultaneous consideration of the relationships between *IS* and *LM* on a plane with axes (Y) and (r) gives just this, the intersection between the two markets. Equilibrium appears at the intersection of the two functions and therefore expresses the *simultaneous* equilibrium of the different markets.

Figure 5.5 reproduces the classic IS-LM model and shows the effects of an interventionist economic policy (government spending). An increase in *G*, government spending (not shown on the graph), causes an increase in investment and savings (*IS*), moving the line up and to the right. The increased investment shows up on the *Y* axis as an increase in income. This also causes an increase in the demand for money, so that at the new equilibrium level, the interest rate is higher as well as the level of income.

Analytically, the IS-LM equations give us a precise quantification of the effects we seek to explain, in this case, aggregate income (*Y*):

$$\Delta Y^* = \frac{1}{1-c + \dfrac{I'}{L'_r} L'_Y} \left[\Delta G + \frac{I'}{L'_r} \Delta M\right].$$

The multiplier thus appears in modified form. Adding a monetary component that expresses the equilibrium conditions of the money market gives us a different multiplier, one that is considerably weaker than the simple multiplier already proposed.

The IS-LM Model and Fixed Prices: Verticalists versus Horizontalists

If the IS-LM model had only one contribution to make, it would be this: it clearly demonstrates that aggregate equilibrium depends on the simultaneous adjustment of many markets. For example, the new part of the multiplier $\left(\dfrac{I'}{L'_r} \cdot L'_y\right)$, in economic terms a *monetary brake*, shows just such market interaction:

- The increase in income that follows an increase in government expenditure (ΔG) causes a tension in the money market. The transaction demand for money increases, and with it the interest rate.
- Simultaneously, the increase in the interest rate weakens private investment, a central component of effective demand.

So, within the confines of this model, the total effect of public expenditure, as measured by the complex multiplier, is less than what we might otherwise expect. Some economists argue that public investment *crowds out*, at least in part, private investment.

Interaction among different markets: such is the message of the IS-LM model. It is also Keynes's message, as has been proved many times. Hicks's work, to this extent, is extremely revealing: it moves Keynesian

thought back in the direction of general equilibrium among many markets. More simply, Hicks reveals fully the Walrasian dimensions of
Keynes's thought.

The IS-LM model, however, is not without critics. More radical readings criticize the model for pushing the *General Theory* backward to the
orthodoxy that it was meant to demolish. First, the IS-LM model is an
extremely mechanical interpretation of the *General Theory;* it forsakes
the essential concept of the economic instabilities that result from uncertainty. Part of the "certainty" of the IS-LM model stems precisely
from its assumption of exogenous money, which separates the money
supply from the investor confidence that is central to the operation of
credit and financial markets. So the second, more serious objection is
linked to the first: in assuming an exogenous supply of money, the
IS-LM model reintroduces the notion of an interest rate that reflects
scarcity. The only novelty here is that with the *LM* money supply curve,
it is the scarcity of *money* that appears as a limiting factor, rather than
the scarcity of *savings* posited by traditional theorists such as Wicksell
and Hayek. The interest rate therefore reappears as an obstacle to economic expansion, and we also lose the notion of a "spending economy"
that Keynes was able to introduce with the novel argument that investment makes savings possible, rather than vice versa.

The quarrel between the pro- and anti–IS-LM positions is captured
in the pithy phrase "verticalists versus horizontalists." On the one hand,
if the *LM* curve is *vertical,* the scarcity of money may be used as a
perfect substitute for the scarcity of savings and we are back in the world
of classical economics and "natural" interest rates. In such a world, public expenditure completely crowds out private investment, and economic
policies are futile. Monetarists, most notably, Milton Friedman, use this
view to oppose expansionist economic policies. This view also requires
a number of assumptions about the slopes of the demand curve, for
money: L'_r must be close to zero, and L'_y very high.

On the other hand, *LM* might be *horizontal.* It could be horizontal
under the assumption of an endogenous money supply, one in which the
banking system makes credit available as businesses ask for it. *LM* could
also be horizontal under the conditions of a "liquidity trap" described
by Keynes. In a liquidity trap, L'_r approaches infinity as the demand for
money for speculative purposes becomes almost infinite. In both of these
"horizontal" cases, a government spending program to spur economic
recovery can be made without affecting the interest rate. The interest

rate does not put a brake on economic recovery, and we are back in the world of the simple multiplier.

The "verticalists versus horizontalists" debate is a crucial dividing line between two great schools of Keynesian interpretation. The *neoclassical synthesis* argues more or less that the IS-LM model adequately represents Keynes's thought. Calculating the elasticities that are associated with I, L'_r and L'_y is therefore the key to determining economic policy. Moreover, one can, thanks to these erudite calculations, hope to diminish the effect of the *monetary brake* that (in this view) accompanies government spending (ΔG) with an expansionary monetary policy (ΔM^s). The artificial (and therefore exogenous) stimulus to the money supply, ΔM^s, is designed to compensate for the scarcity of money and the increase in the interest rate. The neoclassical synthesis underlies the notion of finding the right "policy mix" of government spending and monetary expansion.

On the other hand, the *radical* (including *post-Keynesian*) interpretations of Keynes challenge the synthesis approach. Their main objection concerns the nature of the "market price" of the interest rate. The scarcity of money, and of financial instruments (credit) in general, is in this view not to be compared to a *market* insufficiency of supply that leads to an increase in prices. Indeed, the very notion of a "market" for money is arguable, because the determination of money's price, the interest rate, is not subject to the usual considerations. The supply of money is not in reality exogenous or costly, and the demand for it can be nearly infinite when the anxiety level of investors is very high. This view of endogenous money explains why Keynes argued in favor of the simple value of the multiplier.

IS-LM *and Flexible Prices: The Patinkin Interpretation*

The IS-LM model is an imperfect interpretation of Keynesian thought. This observation, however, does not lessen the model's interest as a tool of economic policy or even as a tool to clarify the *General Theory*, which is a complex and at times contradictory work. So, in spite of its inadequacies, we will not discard the Hicks-Hansen IS-LM model. Moreover, in addition to the simple version we have presented, there are many extensions of the IS-LM model that further justify our interest in it. In particular, the integration of changes in general price levels helps us better understand the relationship that Keynes established between the interest rate, prices, and unemployment.

To incorporate flexible prices into the IS-LM model, we must first explain the role of prices in market equilibriums. Let us see how *IS* and *LM* are modified. Our customary variables (*Y* for income, *C* for consumption, *I* for investment, etc.) are now considered as measuring real values (deflated from their nominal variations). So we obtain new equations distinct from those we have already introduced, denoting them with the subscript 2:

$$pY = p_c(Y) + p_i(r) + p_g \qquad (IS_2)$$

$$\frac{M^s}{P} = \frac{M^d}{P} = L(Y,r) \qquad (LM_2)$$

The accounting equilibrium in the market of goods and services (IS_2) integrates price levels. We make here a simplifying assumption: the price level of consumption goods, p_c, and the price level of investment, p_I, and the price level of public sector consumption goods, p_G, all develop together in such a way that we may take them as equal: $p_c = p_I = p_G = p$. The money market equilibrium is written in terms of real values. To the right, the real demand for money is a function of real income (the transaction motive) and of the real interest rate (the speculative motive). We attribute to agents a rationality similar to the real balance effect posited by Pigou, but we nonetheless keep a very Keynesian element by showing the sensitivity of L, the demand for money, to the rate of interest.

The two-equation system (IS_2) (LM_2) now yields three unknown values, *r*, *Y*, and *p* (the rate of interest, aggregate income, and the price level). Adding a *supply component* will, however, remove this mathematical indeterminacy. To do this we must observe how businesses react to changes in the price level. We get two relationships:

$$Y = F(N)$$

and

$$\frac{w_o}{p} = F'(N) \cdot = F'(N).$$

The first relationship links the sum of all goods produced to the quality of labor set in motion (*N*). This is a simplified production function. The second relationship takes up again the "first classical postulate" (postulate P1 on p. 101): the marginal productivity of labor

$F'(N)$ is equal to the real wage level w_o/p. This last equation adds a profitability criterion to business's decisions to produce goods. In the simple IS-LM model, the only requirement is the presence of demand. We know, however, that profit considerations are not missing from Keynes's thinking: he accepted the first classical postulate, and the principle of effective demand explicitly describes a profit calculation. Integrating a supply component to the IS-LM model therefore appears consistent with Keynes's own thinking.

The partial resolution of the supply component gives us the following:

$$Y = F(F^{-1}\frac{w_o}{p}) = Z(p), \qquad \text{with } Z' > 0.$$

We can therefore write an aggregate supply function Z in a very simplified form, as the sole function of price levels. The supply function Z increases: an increase in prices reduces the real salary, costs diminish, and supply increase. Emphasis must be given, however, to a central assumption of this model: the nominal wage level w_o is presumed rigid, so that changes in real salary are due to changes in price levels (the denominator), and not to changes in nominal wage level, w_o. This presumed rigidity guarantees, without ambiguity, the sensitivity of aggregate supply to price levels.

We may now write the complete differentiated model:

$$\Delta Y (1 - c) = I' \, \Delta r + \Delta G \qquad (IS_2')$$

$$L'_Y \, \Delta Y = \frac{M^s}{p}[\frac{\Delta M^s}{M^s} \ \frac{\Delta p}{p}] \ L'_r \Delta r \qquad (LM_2')$$

$$\Delta Y = Z' \, \Delta p \qquad (\text{Supply})$$

There are two customary ways to resolve this model. We may, as we have already done with the rigid price version of the *IS-LM*, use first (IS_2') to look at variations in income after eliminating variations in the interest rate. Mathematically, it is sufficient to substitute in (IS_2') the value of the interest rate given by (LM_2'). We thereby obtain an aggregate demand function, which shows a decreasing slope when graphed on a plane with axes (p, Y). The intersection of this function with the aggregate supply function Z gives us the equilibrium level and allows us to observe the effects of economic policy. The economic policies of government spending (ΔG) and expansionary monetary policy (ΔM^s) in this scenario show genuine beneficial effects in stimulating the economy, but part of the economic stimulus is lost to an increase in price levels. These inflationary effects can be measured precisely as a function of elasticities in the slopes of the curves.

This method of resolving the equations is used in macroeconomics. It is the AS-AD model, for aggregate supply and aggregate demand.

However, in the interest of understanding Keynes better, we will look at a different method, that proposed by Don Patinkin (1922–1995). Patinkin (1956) proposed substituting in the two equations (IS_2') and (LM_2') the expression of ΔY given by Z, which yields:

$$Z\Delta p\,(1 - c)\ =\ I'\,\Delta r + \Delta G \qquad\qquad (IS\text{pat})$$

and

$$L'_Y\,Z'\,\Delta p = \frac{M^s}{p}[\frac{\Delta M^s}{M^s} - \frac{\Delta p}{p}] - L'_r\,\Delta r \qquad\qquad (LM\text{pat}).$$

We thus know how to calculate on a new plane with axes (p, r) the direction of change in IS and LM in a way that incorporates the supply component. Following assumptions about the partial derivatives, we can also show that the IS curve is a decreasing function, the LM curve an increasing one. The aggregate equilibrium is therefore by two prices (p^*, r^*), called the *dual equilibrium.* The determination of these prices rigorously defines the determination of the real equilibrium on Y, I, and so on, and calculating one is as good as calculating the other.

The interest of this argument appears when we associate the *dual equilibrium* with the calculation of the wage rate and the labor market. Let us first look at the model's Keynesian assumptions.

Let us follow the direction determined by the model as indicated by the arrows. The intersection of IS and LM on the plane with axes (r, p) in Figure 5.6a determines an equilibrium interest rate and also an equilibrium price level. At a constant nominal wage level, this equilibrium level determines the real wage (w_o/p), which appears on the axis in Figure 5.6b. Then, in accordance with the first classical postulate, the real wage determines, on the demand side, the quantity of labor actually put to work, as shown in Figure 5.6c.

Figure 5.6   **Patinkin's Interpretation: The Dual Determination (p^*, r^*)**

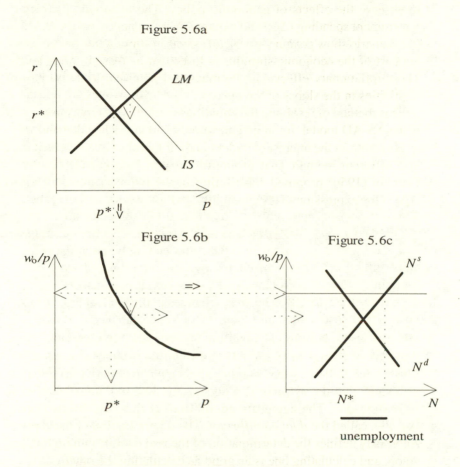

Figure 5.6a

Figure 5.6b

Figure 5.6c

unemployment

As shown in the three diagrams, the initial equilibrium position is one of involuntary unemployment: the intersection of *IS* and *LM* in Figure 5.6a sets 5.6b such that in Figure 5.6c the real wage is too high for everyone who wants a job to be employed. Following some kind of stimulus (government spending or monetary expansion), the *IS* curve shifts up and to the right in Figure 5.6a. Following the small arrows, we see that the resulting *increase* in the interest rate and price levels in Figure 5.6a has the immediate effect of *lowering the real wage,* as shown in Figure 5.6b. This lowered wage makes employers more willing to hire and also causes some workers to withdraw from the labor market. The demand for labor is increased, and the supply, at the new, lower wage level, is decreased. The downward movement of the wage level line in Figure 5.6c brings the wage level to precisely the point where N^s, the supply of labor, and N^d, the demand for labor, intersect. At that point, we have reached a full-employment equilibrium in Patinkin's model.

This interpretation turns the Keynesian model into an extremely cynical theory. That does not mean it is wrong, however. Wages are outrun by inflation, and workers are led to accept, in spite of themselves, a lower real wage. It is precisely this lowering of the real wage that allows unemployment to be reduced. We should also add that this theoretical result received some empirical corroboration in the famous *Phillips curve*, which followed observations that there was a decreasing relationship between inflation and unemployment (higher inflation led to more jobs). That, at least, is what appeared statistically in the developed countries in the 1950s and 1960s. So in practice, at least during this period, it appeared that lower unemployment rates could be purchased at the price of higher inflation (the famous unemployment-inflation trade-off).

Patinkin's interpretation of the IS-LM model has been much discussed. It accentuates the interaction between changes in the general price level and wage rigidity, and integrates them into a Keynesian model. But does this interpretation of the *IS-LM* really work as a valid interpretation of the *General Theory?* Clearly, we lose much of the subtlety of Keynes's arguments: quantitative adjustments in employment and price levels, as a function of entrepreneurial expectations, are lost in the dual couple relationship of (p^* and r^*). Above all, a first reading of Figures 5.6a, b, and c leads us again (as did, in another way, Hicks) to the "New Keynesian Economics" position that at bottom is purely classical: unemployment is caused by excessively high real wages, and therefore these must be reduced. The only difference is the means offered: Patinkin would have us lower the wage level by increasing the denominator of the nominal price level, p, in the real wage level (w_o/p), whereas classical theory recommends reducing the nominal wage in the numerator, w_o.

It is this last thought, in combination with a close rereading of Chapter 2 of the *General Theory,* that gives Patinkin's interpretation of the IS-LM model its pertinence. We are to some extent covering ground we have covered before; the reader may wish to refer to our discussion in Chapter 4 of this book, from the beginning up to the discussion of Figures 4.1 and 4.2. Indeed, the last figure of Patinkin's version of *IS-LM*, Figure 5.6c, is identical to Figure 4.2.

Figure 5.7 **Patinkin's Interpretation: The Classical Cause**

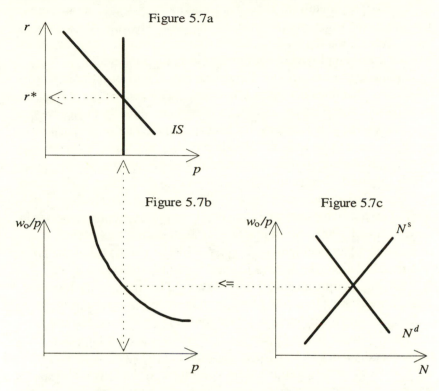

So just what is Keynes telling us in Chapter 2 of the *General Theory?* First, he is telling us that the starting point of unemployment is false prices: a real wage level set such that it does not permit the use of all labor factors (full employment). But then he tells us that it would be feckless to modify the nominal wage without, at the same time, taking into account the simultaneous determination of prices. The price level, therefore, is not independent of the wage level.

We recall that in the *General Theory* the principle of effective demand sets the price level; in Patinkin's graph, this principle takes the following form: the price level is set at the intersection point of *IS* and *LM*. That is, Patinkin explicitly integrates a monetary blockage (*LM*) into his determination of the real level of equilibrium (*IS*).

On the contrary, in Figure 5.7, the classical version of Patinkin's graph shows, working backward from the equilibrium employment level, that Keynes's predecessors all tried to deny the existence of this blockage.

In Figure 5.7c, the equilibrium employment level is shown, setting an equilibrium price and wage level in Figure 5.7b (following the arrow). The price level in 5.7b in turn determines the level of *I-S* equality in Figure 5.7a and the interest rate.

In the classical conception, the lack of demand for money for speculative purposes ($L'_r = 0$) makes the *LM* curve (the supply and demand for money) totally insensitive to the real interest rate. This is not necessarily a constraint: under these conditions, for Keynes, the order of causality shifts from the money to the labor market, whereas in the classical model it shifts from the labor market to the interest rate. The absence of an *LM* curve *leaves the price level free,* so that the real wage reaches its equilibrium level with the labor market. In other words, monetary factors do not constitute a constraint on achieving real equilibrium, and we find anew the classical world of a perfect dichotomy between monetary phenomena and the real economy.

Equilibrium in the Keynesian model, to the contrary, is affected by money. Effective demand is sensitive to monetary phenomena. Graphed on the plane with axes (p, r), it is the constraining force of the *LM* curve, which did not exist in classical economics, that shows the effects of monetary phenomena. A degree of freedom has been removed from the model, and this removal impedes the adjustment between the interest rate and the price level. The sensitivity of the demand for bank deposits to the rate of interest is the fundamental innovation, which Keynes invented in breaking with the classical theorists. This is the raison d'être of the *LM* curve. This leads us to the following interpretation of Keynes: the distortion of wages (rigidity of w_o, the nominal wage) is not a problem unless it is accompanied by a monetary distortion as well, a particular version of the real balance effect linked to the interest rate.

And this is Patinkin's point.

Conclusion: Synthesizing Keynes?

This chapter has focused on the macroeconomic adjustment process. The questions Keynes asks have been inserted into an older logic, that of the equilibrium between savings and investment. Keynes's ingenious response, a posteriori savings, opens up any number of possibilities for extension. Following tradition, we have set forward some of the generations of thinking that came after Keynes. The analyses of the *General Theory* led the economics discipline to a new method, that of modern macroeconomics. This method, using simplified models, consists in observing the intersecting adjustment of the most important markets in the economy. The IS-LM model is the most famous symbol of this new path. It reintegrates the question of the savings-investment adjustment into a Walrasian perspective of general market equilibrium (to do so, the *IS-LM* simplifies "a posteriori savings" to the orthodox meaning of "savings that occur after the market of goods and services has adjusted").

Keynes's achievement, in light of these views of the IS-LM model, has been reduced to a mere borrowing, however brilliant and relevant, of the Marshallian (and Pigovian) views on general equilibrium. Due to the IS-LM model's powerful influence, commentators have even discussed the neoclassical incorporation of Keynesian analysis, itself an indication of the degree to which the IS-LM model strains to find compatibility between the Keynesian and classical systems of analysis. The neoclassical synthesis school tries to bridge this gap: neoclassical analysis is valid for the values of certain economic parameters (L'_r, L'_y, . . .), Keynesian analysis for others; but the same model is used.

Is the neoclassical synthesis a betrayal of Keynes's thought or a judicious distillation of Keynes's views, which in the end seem to bristle with more radical innovations than they have in reality? This is the question to which we now turn.

Note

1. If people voluntarily increase savings, this is not a problem in Hayek's model, but his discussion focuses on an involuntary increase in savings as a result of monetary policy.

6

Five Readings of Keynes

What should we take away from our exploration of Keynes's work? There is no single answer. Our political beliefs, our adherence to one or another school of economics, and even our social position are among the factors that cause us to emphasize, in our own interpretations, this or that element of Keynes's message. There are many possible readings of Keynes, and many theoretical extensions that exploit the various doors he opened.

Although in the literal sense there are as many interpretations of Keynes as there are readers, we have selected five different theoretical positions as the principal stars in the constellation of Keynesian analysis.

The First "Synthesis": *IS-LM* and Its Extensions

The IS-LM model remains the first great movement in the interpretation of Keynes's thought. It began with Hicks's article, "Mr. Keynes and the Classics: A Suggested Interpretation," published in *Econometrica* (1937). As mentioned in the previous chapter, Hicks's basic ideas were further developed into the Hicks-Hansen IS-LM model with Hansen's contributions (1949, 1953).

The IS-LM model owes its success to very different factors. The first reason is that it became available very early to clarify the message of the *General Theory*. Keynes's text is often opaque. His style of argument presents a number of perhaps deliberate ambiguities. The IS-LM model tried to erase these ambiguities. The result was a highly selective interpretation whose principal virtue was its clarity and simplicity. In the short term, it was the ready and easy way to get immediate access to Keynes's thought.

The second reason for the success of the hydraulic synthesis of Keynes's thought is that the IS-LM model and its extensions were indispensable tools for economic policy analysis throughout the 1950s and 1960s. With the introduction of flexible prices into the model (as we have seen with Patinkin's work in the previous chapter), econometric modeling based on the IS-LM's assumptions had the immense advantage of sticking very closely to the Phillips curve trade-off between inflation and unemployment.[1] In other words, the model was vindicated in practical use because the data of that period seemed to support it. We remark, too, that Keynes himself had paved the road to this interpretation, because in Chapter 2 of the *General Theory* he insisted on the equivalence postulate, that is, the linkage between changes in the real wage level and changes in the level of unemployment (see Chapter 4 of this book).

Nonetheless, today the IS-LM reading of Keynes is controverted. The post-Keynesian school, for example, refers to it negatively. Paul Davidson (1994, 118), disparages the IS-LM model as "a failed representation of Keynes." Moreover, the Phillips curve is no longer empirically verified. Even so, well before stagflation of the 1970s, not long even after 1937, it became fashionable to challenge the supposed virtues of the hydraulic interpretations of Keynes. Economists strove to present their own interpretations, and even John Hicks eventually jumped into the game (see his *Causality in Economics* 1979). The extent to which the IS-LM model fails to capture Keynesian thought will be discussed again later in this chapter. Much depends, in the end, on the uses to which the model is put. In this section, however, we would like to defend the *IS-LM* against a straw man argument that to us seems inaccurate.

We often hear that, in the hydraulic versions of Keynes, the role attributed to uncertainty is insufficient. But this *insufficiency* all too often, and all too hastily, is reduced to *nonexistence*. It is just a step from insufficiency to nonexistence, but it is a step we do not wish to take. The IS-LM model incorporates uncertainty in its own particular way, to be sure. But uncertainty is there.

To convince ourselves that uncertainty is in fact present in the IS-LM model, we need only reconsider briefly the construction of its monetary component. The sensitivity of the demand for money to the interest rate results from investors' uncertainty about future changes in the interest rate. This uncertainty in fact determines the slope of the *LM* (money demand, money supply) curve. Investors' reaction to uncertainty constrains the adjustment process and therefore explains, at the intersection of the *IS* and *LM* curves, the equilibrium level of income. In other words, in the IS-LM model, uncertainty about the monetary environment reduces effective demand below the full employment level.

It is also true, however, that some neoclassical-synthesis Keynesian works have sought to minimize the role of uncertainty in determining the demand for money. They find other justifications for the interest rate's influence, such as Tobin's analyses of transaction costs (Tobin 1956, 1958, 1968). That does not alter, however, the fact that the research program opened by Keynes was based on the relationship between money and uncertainty.

The Post-Keynesians

The post-Keynesians, as their name indicates, see their work as an immediate continuation of the *General Theory*. During the 1930s, Keynes had a small group of readers for his work before it went out for publication. This group was baptized "the Circus." The work of other members, including Richard Kahn (1905–1989), E.A.G. Robinson (1897–1994), Joan Robinson (1903–1983), and Piero Sraffa (1898–1983), was also discussed. It was in this intimate circle that the multiplier concept was perfected. The members of the Circus stayed in Cambridge. But the club grew larger, taking on new members in Cambridge and elsewhere. It came to be referred to as the Cambridge School, but to be more inclusive, the post-Keynesian label was also used. During the 1950s and 1960s, the post-Keynesians sought to extend the fundamental principles of the *General Theory* to economic subjects that Keynes, under pressure to publish in response to the economic crisis of his time, could not consider in 1936.

As summarized by Paul Davidson (1994), the dean of American post-Keynesianism, the Cambridge School's work has three main points on which it challenges the three principal axioms of traditional neoclassical theory.

1. *First contested axiom.* Post-Keynesians deny the perfect substitutability of goods, or production factors. The real world is not as flexible as classical theory supposes. For example, the Cobb-Douglas production function, where labor may instantly be substituted for capital according to the relative cost of the two factors, is for the Cambridge School a pure fiction. Indeed, "capital" itself is too abstract a term to be brought into the discussion. The Cambridge School proposes models of

the economy in which the substitution of capital for labor (and vice versa) is imperfect. On this basis, a post-Keynesian theory of growth can be developed. The *General Theory* described short-term equilibrium and crisis unemployment. Could its principles be extended to the long term? The debate was launched by Ray F. Harrod (1900–1978) and Evsey Domar (1914–1997) whose combined work (Harrod, 1939, 1948; Domar, 1946) became known as the Harrod-Domar growth model. These efforts influenced other Cambridge School members to consider the relationship between distribution of income and growth. In their work, flexibility in the distribution of income replaced the flexibility of the production function. Starting with the observation that different groups in the economy have different marginal propensities to save, could a distribution of income from one group to another improve the aggregate growth in the economy? Kaldor (1908–1986), Joan Robinson, and Luigi Pasinetti (1930–) worked in this area (Kaldor 1954, 1956, 1961, 1962; Robinson 1956, 1962; Pasinetti 1962, 1974). Sraffa (1960) even elaborated the remarkable congruence of this line of thinking with Ricardo's development model.

2. *Second contested axiom.* Post-Keynesians deny that we live in an ergodic world, where the expectation of agents may rationally be modeled even though the world is full of risky, uncertain events. The erudite jargon phrase, an *ergodic world,* contains assumptions about the nature of uncertainty, and uncertainty's effects on the real economy. Chance events can lead to economic disturbances because an unexpected shock affects all elements of the economy. Will the economy stabilize after these disturbances, or will they produce a truly chaotic movement that is altogether uncontrollable and unforeseeable? In the first case, that of an ergodic world where an unforeseen shock disturbs the economy but ultimately stabilizes, we can consider the existence of equilibrium and the development of rational expectations about what the equilibrium level will be. In the second case, the post-Keynesian, *nonergodic* world, reality is unintelligible to the extent that it is anarchic. Under these conditions, it seems impossible to believe that economic agents can have any rational expectations whatsoever about reality and its future evolution. The post-Keynesian, nonergodic position points clearly to a radical revision of classical theories about the behavior of agents in an uncertain universe. This is a rallying point of post-Keynesians generally. One of the leaders in the domain of uncertainty was G.L.S. Shackle (1903–1992) (see, for example, Shackle 1955, 1990).

3. *Third contested axiom.* Post-Keynesian theorists argue that money is nonneutral. In an uncertain economy, where adjustment processes are imperfect, money acquires properties wholly different from those associated with classical models. Post-Keynesians deny the most important of these classical properties, the neutrality of money. Following Keynes, they argue that nonneutrality is manifested through the interest rate. Another important element of money, *liquidity* and its effects on uncertainty, are for the post-Keynesians completely central to understanding monetary phenomena. The instability of financial markets and the impact of liquidity preference have been the object of detailed study, especially by Hyman P. Minsky (1919–1997) and Paul Davidson (1930–), (see for example, Minsky 1982; Davidson 1994).

The Circuit School

Another, more recently established school of Keynesian interpretation has focused on the question of money and subjected it to particularly detailed analysis. The circuit school (from the French *circuit*, emphasizing the notion of current or flow) has focused principally on the question of a *monetary economy*. In such an economy, money can no longer be considered the *n*th good (bought and sold as an intermediate for the exchange process). Money appears instead as the essential support of the flow of goods. It is the channel that conveys all other goods. The major members of this school are French or Québécois: Alain Parguez (1987, 1996), F. Poulon (1985, 1987), Bernard Schmitt (1988, 1996), and Marc Lavoie (1997, 1999). Lavoie has produced a useful summary of the circuitist work to date and its future agenda (1992). The characteristic lines of inquiry of this school follow.

1. Circuitism's first line of inquiry concerns the status of money, as has just been described above. The circuitists have a novel concept of money supply and the manner in which the economy is financed. The principle of effective demand that links aggregate supply and demand, as well as investment and savings, must additionally, by symmetry, identify the supply and demand for money. The concrete mechanism of this identity is credit, which assures businesses the simultaneous creation of a value (created by investment) and of a vehicle for this value (money). In other words, the money supply is endogenous and necessarily adjusts to demand. The circuit theory challenges even the use of supply and demand: if there is a strict identity of these two concepts, then money

cannot really have a market. It is in the heart of bankers' accounting ledgers that these circuits are opened and closed. The interest rate, in this line of thinking, is not an objective price.

2. This view of the interest rate causes circuitist theorists to focus on the finance motive, where investor and banker meet. This is the logical condition for a truly *endogenous* money supply. The finance motive may be defined as a fourth reason for holding money (the other three, we remember, are speculation, transactions, and liquidity: see pp. 116–120). Where credit exists, it describes the means by which entrepreneurs have succeeded in financing their investment through monetary creation. As we have said before, the consideration of this fact constitutes the most pertinent criticism one can make of the IS-LM construct, because it destroys one of the two pillars of the model. That is, it denies the "crowding-out" effect linked to increases in the interest rate. We have seen this earlier in our discussion of horizontalism in the previous chapter. Either money is exogenous, as in the IS-LM model, and crowding-out effects are almost as limiting on the economy as in the pure classical tradition, or money is endogenous, so crowding-out effects do not exist because the interest rate need not vary. What is at stake in the finance motive is the rejection of *scarcity* as the objective principle in economic regulation and a push for the truly heterodox nature of Keynesian economics. As long as the interest rate remains a price that signals pressure on resources, Keynesian economics is in the end a vague variation on neoclassical economics and its scarce money. On the other hand, as soon as the interest rate is abolished from this role, the Keynesian system is completely freed from its classical roots. The finance motive in the *General Theory* is nonetheless an underused idea, as if Keynes had not understood that it was essential to the radical theoretical construct he was building. The finance motive, as used by the circuit school, was not systematically used by Keynes until two articles he published in 1937, "The 'Ex-Ante' Theory of the Rate of Interest," and "Alternative Theories of the Rate of Interest." After these articles, the interest rate becomes eminently subjective in character. Formerly, it had been an objective signal of tensions in the competition for scarce resources; after 1937, it became the quasi-prophetic messenger of the financial system. In other words, the interest rate measures the degree of disconnection between the real sphere of production and the financial sphere.

3. The last major aspect of circuitist theory is its methodology. Its fundamental postulates of economic inquiry are specific to it, which is

why it has its name. The circuit school is above all else a macroeconomic school; microeconomic analysis, relationships in the market, is a second-tier consideration. The circuit school even challenges all references to market equilibrium, because economic reality is held to have one major source, the circulation of goods. This position has its roots in a refusal to accept the notion of time and temporal periods. In a representation of time in successive periods, t_1, t_2, t_3 ... t_n, one can talk about a clearing of accounts in each period and hence an equilibrium in the neoclassical sense. But if one looks at time differently, as the circuitists do, and sees that historical time consists of successive decisions that are balanced by the "clearing of markets" a posteriori, then the concept of equilibrium has to be reexamined.

As a general rule, the theses of the circuit school challenge the validity of the habitual categories used by economists, especially the standard representations of instantaneous accounting equilibriums (as, for example, in the IS-LM model, where a change in *IS* instantaneously changes *LM,* and vice versa). Circuitism is a truly *heterodox* approach to economics. Its major concepts are formed, so to speak, upstream from the usual scientific methods. This is its strength, but also its weakness, and proponents of this approach are struggling to get broader mainstream attention to their ideas.

The Second Synthesis: The New Keynesian Economics

Another school of thought, much more widely recognized in academics, is the New Keynesian Economics (NKE). This fourth current has had many contributors over the decades. In its early days it was sometimes called disequilibrium theory or the theory of fixed-price equilibrium. Two major writers in this tradition of Keynesian thought, Clower (1969) and Leijonhuvfud (1968), were also responsible for its name. The theory sought, on the basis of insights first advanced by Keynes, to reintroduce money into the Walrasian perspective on general equilibrium. Where *false prices* are present, money loses its neutrality because markets fail to clear. We have mentioned false prices in a number of places (see index). The NKE school focuses directly on this and related questions; its general thesis is that Walrasian general equilibrium, minus its fictional auctioneer and perfect price flexibility, is the best framework with which to reinterpret Keynesian theory.

The main preoccupations of NKE analysis are monetary questions and why prices are false. At the end of the 1960s and the beginning of the 1970s, the theory of rational expectations challenged many traditional Keynesian assumptions and policy instruments. An article by Lucas (1976) showed the ineffectiveness of monetary policy, and another by Barro (1974) showed the ineffectiveness of fiscal policy. As a group, these contributions sought to invalidate the most mechanistic versions of Keynesian macroeconomics. They focused on the neutralization, by the anticipations of private parties, of government efforts to manipulate economic activity. Lucas and Barro pointed out that such manipulations can succeed only if changes in prices outstrip the ability of agents to anticipate them.

The New Keynesian Economics may be construed as a reaction to the "new classical economics" (NCE) of Lucas and Barro. The use of the word "new" in both titles indicates the direct rivalry between the NCE and NKE schools. Specifically, the NKE school integrated and assimilated the criticisms of the rational expectations school. What was at stake was finding the microeconomic foundations of Keynesian macroeconomics: individual behaviors and efforts to anticipate the future had be observed and explained. The major names of the NKE school have international reputations. These theorists include Akerlof (1986), Azariadis (1975), Benassy (1975, 1976, 1984, 1993), Blanchard and Kiyotaki (1987), Gordon (1990), Malinvaud (1977, 1980), Mankiw and Romer (1991), and Stiglitz (1984); with Greenwald 1997; with Weiss 1981).

The central argument of the NKE school is that even in the presence of rational expectations of agents, the concrete processes of price formation in markets are inefficient. Markets fail in their role of efficiently allocating resources. These market failures have been shown to result from *endogenous* (built-in, and thus, perhaps, inescapable) price rigidities, rather than the assumed price rigidities that earlier characterized the neoclassical synthesis of Keynesian thought. Most of the time, weaknesses in the pricing system are due to imperfect information available to agents. Information is costly to obtain, where it is not lacking altogether. "Adverse selection" (hidden information) and "moral hazard" (due to hidden behaviors) impose costs on transactions and disturb the process by which contracts are made. The work of the NKE school touched upon every sector of the economy: the labor market, the financial market, and the markets for goods and services.

Following a line of thought developed much earlier by Joan Robinson (1932) and Chamberlin (1933), NKE theorists also took into account industrial organization. They sought an explanation for different degrees of pricing flexibility in ententes among firms and among workers (as a part of union activity). These avenues then led NKE theorists to disconnect prices from their function of signaling changes in the economy. In the absence of price coordination, these theorists considered alternative forms of coordination. "Coordination failures" are a key element of the economy. Coordination failures result from the lack of efficient markets and from the strategic interactions that replace them. Agents' individual efforts fail to coordinate themselves, collectively, in a way that achieves a satisfactory equilibrium (see Cooper and John 1988).

The NKE school also analyzes market *incompleteness* as well as market imperfection. Fundamentally, entrepreneurs face economic uncertainty in the moment that they themselves determine effective demand because there is no insurance market for system-wide unsold inventory. Entrepreneurs can protect their goods against fires, but not against a general failure to sell. The lack of such insurance is, in fact, the reason that uncertainty exists. The lack of such insurance also helps explain Keynes's preference for consumption and antipathy to savings. Savings, as deferred consumption, leave a large degree of uncertainty hovering over the economy. The *incompleteness of markets,* the fact that there is no complete system of contingent markets (goods markets for the present and the future), is therefore the basic cause of uncertainty.

As a result, the NKE school takes an interest in the properties of financial markets that tend to reduce incompleteness. Under certain conditions, a forward market of financial products (stocks, bonds, futures, and other securities) provides reasonable insurance and is a good substitute for contingent markets. In other situations, uncertainty remains: the macroeconomic equilibrium can be reached at any of a number of different levels. "Multiple equilibriums" are therefore possible. Azariadis and Guesnerie (1986), Guesnerie and Woodford (1992), Farmer (1993), and Grandmont (1986) have worked on these problems. At bottom, these efforts are a perfect synthesis of the line of inquiry that runs between Keynesian macroeconomics and neoclassical thinking about Walrasian general equilibrium, as applied to uncertainty.

Interpretations Based on Radical Uncertainty

The four schools of thought that we have summarized so far have one point in common: they stress the role of uncertainty in Keynesian theory.

Of course, the degree of emphasis varies in each school. The definition of uncertainty itself shifts from school to school. In one, it is the lack of information; in another, it is "radical," which is to say, linked to the definition advanced earlier by Knight (1921). In Chapter 3 of this book, we recall, Knight's uncertainty related to a universe in which probabilities could not be estimated, whereas Keynes referred to the degree of "weight" that could be attributed to probabilistic reasoning. "Radical uncertainty" is considered by some theorists as the fundamental key to the interpretation of Keynes's work. Taken together, these authors are sufficiently cohesive to constitute a school.

Reading Keynes's work through the lens of radical uncertainty results first of all from Keynes's own writings. He himself seemed to give to his thinking the dimensions of a true "general theory of uncertainty." To this end, two texts are of central importance: Chapter 12 of the *General Theory* and the fifteen-page article "The General Theory of Employment," (1937), in which Keynes sums up some of the principal arguments of the book of 1936. Both texts provide a vision of an economic behavior in a world where agents are permeated with the uncertainty that surrounds them. Keynes to some extent picks up on ideas already developed in the *Treatise on Probability,* as we have seen in Chapter 3 of this book. Uncertainty is defined by the minimal weight attached to logical reasoning (weights approach zero). Rational ways to interpret real conditions, much less foresee them, are not only difficult to validate but infrequently used by agents. Without a stable base on which to construct expectations, other rules of behavior develop.

In Chapter 12 of the *General Theory,* Keynes limits the field of uncertainty to behavior in financial markets. In the "General Theory of Employment" (1937), the behavior is extended to the entire economy, which becomes a vast "casino." In such circumstances, according to Keynes, reasonable investors are merely trying to save face by appearing reasonable to other investors. There are three ways to do this:

1. Pretend that the present is the best guide to the future and that there will be no radical breaks between the present and the future;
2. Pretend that people around us have a more correct opinion of the future;
3. And so conform to the average public opinion—that is to say, act conventionally.

Thus, the word is out: *convention*. Keynes himself proposes one of the keys to understanding his work. It is a theory of economic behavior that is fundamentally affected by the uncertainty of the environment. Traditional rationality (individual collection and analysis of information, forecasting, decision, and then action) does not apply. The new rule is: follow convention. In Chapter 12 (*CW* 7:156), Keynes compares the behavior of players in securities markets to a type of beauty contest popular in the 1930s. Participants must pick "the six prettiest faces from a hundred photographs, the prize being awarded to the competitor whose choice most nearly corresponds to the average preferences of the competitors as a whole." The value of securities lies in the value that other investors attach to them. To make a good choice in buying a stock or bond, it is not a question of finding the best-performing company, but the one whose price will best move because of the favorable views of other investors. "Worldly wisdom teaches that it is better for reputation to fail conventionally than to succeed unconventionally" (*CW* 7:158).

Thus defined, behavior in financial markets is *self-referential*. Investors worry about what their reference group thinks, not about "external" considerations such as the health of the enterprise (or even government) to which they entrust their money. Without any anchor in reality, the price of securities can substantially differ from their fundamental value, as indicated by the health of the enterprise. The very fact of this split between "real" and "market" value leads to still more uncertainty. Self-referential finance activity becomes more important than real economic activity; speculative bubbles appear, notwithstanding the presence of agents with "rational expectations." It becomes easy to envision a financial crash or panic. A high interest rate and weak fundamentals in the economy become concrete manifestations of the essential instability of markets.

So, when explaining his own book to others, Keynes insists a great deal on the *casino economy*. Many later works have taken up this idea and tried to develop it further. André Orléan (1992) and Jean-Pierre Dupuy (1992) have tried to illuminate the linkages and discontinuities that exist between the assumption of a "conventional actor" as opposed to the "rational actor" of classical economic theory. Is imitation rational? To what extent does mimicry inject a collective dimension into the rational individualism of neoclassical models? Are these apparently antagonistic views somehow complementary? A *theory of convention* is taking shape under these considerations. Members of this school include

Eymard-Duvernay and Bessy (1997), Favereau (1985), Thévenot (1993; with Livet 1994). The idea is to show that in addition to a market that coordinates individual decisions, there are other forms of coordinated behavior of economic agents. Conventions, as established by individuals or groups, appear as a form of economic regulation, another accounting process to which individual decisions are subjected. Conventions may be favorable, or they may be unfavorable, reinforcing the weak underlying condition of the economy. This is, of course, reminiscent of Keynes's "state of confidence."

At the macroeconomic level, the government and its policies are the highest of conventions: in principle, actions of the state may reduce uncertainty, but its ability and aptitude for doing so depend on idiosyncratic factors (its decision makers) and structural factors (the degree to which the state represents society). These factors condition the credibility of state action and, in the end, its efficacy. Moreover, the state's organizational and regional structure may be as important as its budgetary and monetary policies. Private activity must sometimes be regulated at the regionally specific level, an area that has been studied by Salais (1999; with Whiteside 1998). At the microeconomic level, again, conventions (the explicit and implicit rules that agents share in the domain of work and finance contracts) determine the efficacy of economic regulation. The anthology edited by Orléan (1992) gives a sample of works in this area. We might truly argue that the "visible fist" of conventions among agents complements the "invisible hand" that regulates markets.

The *constructivist* reading of Keynes fits well with the *conventionalist* interpretation alluded to in Chapter 4 of this book (especially pp. 115, 128–129) in the discussion of effective demand (these ideas are further explored in Ventelou 2001 and Ventelou 2002). By reversing the *S-I* relationship (see Chapter 5), Keynes opens the conceptual road to an economy that is no longer constrained by physical scarcity. Natural resource endowments no longer determine the level of economic activity. Rather, resources are in the domain of human decision making; it is humans who, in the act of placing bets on their own future, invent the need for resources and finally end up making them. In the conventionalist view, many of economics' most sacred variables, even those at the heart of the IS-LM model, are subject to reinterpretation. The demand for money and its corollary, interest; the marginal efficiency of capital, and its corollary, investment; the level of effective demand and its corollary, employment—all are understood as *conventional* measures of a community's subjective, and by that fact, objective, willingness to put itself to work. The result is that neither the level of economic activity nor the employment rate reflects, as in classical economics, "the natural." The natural interest rate, the natural resource endowment, the natural rate of profit, the natural price of goods, the natural rate of compensation for labor, and the most recent shibboleth, the natural rate of unemployment, all disappear. They are mere false constructs and preconceptions, carried in people's heads and manifested in their behavior.

The conventionalist approach to Keynesianism, in eliminating "the natural" from economic regulation, privileges instead the human will. As a society, we are invited to *realize* our goals in the way that we prefer, rather than suffer as the powerless servants of natural laws that somehow always seem to require poverty, maldistribution, and the hopelessness and waste that are part of joblessness. To borrow from more orthodox terminology, the "natural order" would seem to tolerate any of a number of multiple possible equilibriums; it is up to socioeconomic agents to make and choose one level as opposed to another.

Surely, therefore, we need not entertain a fatalistic resignation to unemployment. We can, and must, act and react, as individuals and as a collectivity, to expunge unemployment, even the very idea of it, from the tool kit of economic regulation. Here, too, the limits are more in our minds than in our bodies; the so-called "natural" constraints are no more than subjective illusions, if we but have the will to see.

Conclusion: The Radical versus the Pragmatic Programs of Keynesian Interpretation

Among the five readings of Keynes that we have just summarized, which is best? There are many answers to the question. First, it is not necessary to limit ourselves to one reading; the interpretations are not, at least in all aspects, mutually exclusive. Sometimes they are complementary. The "second synthesis," or New Keynesian Economics, completes and refines the "first synthesis," the neoclassical synthesis of the Hicks-Hansen IS-LM model. The microeconomic foundations of the NKE school, with its emphasis on market failures and price rigidities, shows the specific conditions under which the old IS-LM model can indeed work. This makes the macroeconomic warhorse of the *IS-LM* more pertinent, not less. In another vein, the circuitist and radical uncertainty theses are not too far apart. Indeed, the circuitist macroeconomic methodology could enrich the more specific considerations of the conventionalist approach.

As a historical proposition, the different readings surveyed here might be divided into two basic camps. Favereau (1985) proposed that the different tendencies might be grouped into those that favor the radical Keynesian project and those that favor the so-called pragmatic project. Both tendencies have their roots in the genesis of the *General Theory* in the years 1930 to 1936. The *radical project* reflects Keynes's ambition, at least until 1933, to revolutionize economic theory from top to bottom. Based on a new concept of uncertainty, Keynesian thought aimed to construct a new economic theory that would be fundamentally incompatible with the traditional theories of economics. Keynes's Chapter 12, written as the *General Theory* was just beginning to take form, is considered a vestigial remnant of the radical project.

The *pragmatic program* is, quite to the contrary, a reorientation of the initial project. This reorientation, which began at the end of 1933, was driven by the need to propose a series of tools that would be immediately useful to debate and convince Keynes's professional contemporaries, especially the classical economists who dominated the policy making of the 1930s. As a result, Keynes sought, after 1934, to minimize his radical ambitions. He made concessions to orthodox doctrine, as seen in Chapter 2 of the *General Theory,* where he argues that unemployment is a market imperfection. Chapter 12, buried in the center of the book, in Favereau's view is a vestige of Keynes's earlier radical project.

It is obviously the pragmatic program of the *General Theory* that serves as the basis of the "synthesis schools" that followed. The efforts of economists such as Hicks, and later Patinkin, follow this tradition. They both sought to make Keynes's intuitions compatible with standard neoclassical methodology. The IS-LM model is the single greatest monument to this effort. At the same time, there remained enough of the radical project in the *General Theory* to beg for subsequent theorists to chip away at the classical strata until at last the radical, abandoned substrate would again see the light of day. Alain Barrère (1985) argues Keynes's work has branches like a family tree, and that the task of ongoing analysis is to understand all the branches. Gradually, such efforts are yielding a generalized Keynesianism that expresses Keynes's overall message. The post-Keynesian, circuitist, and radical uncertainty schools are all major efforts along these lines.

The present chapter has sought to explain, so far as is possible, the pragmatic and radical versions of Keynes with equal emphasis. I have not sought to say which is better, but I do have two remarks. First, there is no systematic opposition between the radical and pragmatic programs. For example, Arrous (1982) observed that the hydraulic and radical conceptions of Keynes might even be complementary: when the state of confidence is stable, that is, when agents' expectations follow an established convention (perhaps more or less optimistic), the position of the curves has no reason to change. So long as a given pattern of convention holds, the hydraulic view is valid. We may, in such cases, apply the IS-LM methodology without risks. It is only when conventions change that the model becomes erroneous.

Second, knowing what we do of Keynes's life and his constant effort to anchor his research agenda in the most concrete aspects of economic life, we perhaps err in seeing his pragmatic program as a forced conversion. All in all, Keynes's pragmatism has served us well. The *General Theory* has enormously changed the science of economics. It gave birth to new questions, especially concerning forecasting the structural processes of change in the economy, and to a new methodology, macroeconomics. Under the *General Theory*'s influence, economics has changed from an abstract and speculative science to an applied discipline that, thanks to measurement and empirical methods, has become an essential tool of economic policy. Perhaps the essence of the Keynesian revolution lies in its methodological project.[2]

Notes

1. The Phillips curve is a statistically observed relationship between the unemployment rate and wage inflation. A "dose" of inflation could "cure" unemployment, and unemployment could "cure" inflation. The stagflation of the 1970s caused problems for this model, but its reasoning is still implicit in reserve banks' policies of raising interest rates to combat rising prices.

2. I have commented elsewhere (Ventelou 1997) that, in 1933, Keynes's methodological concerns drew him closer to the philosophy of Wittgenstein. Their reciprocal influences on one another may even have led to a simultaneous conversion in that year.

7

Keynes

Daring in Policy and Intellect

It is an understatement to say that Keynes's work is immensely rich. The multiple schools of interpretation, half a century after his death, are proof of this. Setting aside the quarrels among rival schools, part of the richness of Keynes's work is that he attracts many different readerships, each of which tends to emphasize, in its own interpretations, different elements of his concerns. The shopworn remark that the disposition of the readers influences the reception of the message is nonetheless very applicable, and it also influences Keynes's impact on the contemporary scene. Today, Keynes enjoys two broad categories of readers: policy makers and academics.

Academics favor Keynes's work for its "density," that is, the fact that his work lends itself to many different readings, interpretations, and theoretical extensions. And it is in academe that the most radical Keynesian projects are found, in the political and theoretical senses. The most far-reaching interpretations focus on Keynes's concept of uncertainty and undermine more traditional "hydraulic" interpretations of his work. The science of economics certainly can benefit from, and even needs, the fresh approaches found in some of the newer interpretations of Keynes. But scholarly arguments should not cause us to lose sight of Keynes's principal message: we need not accept the inevitability of unemployment, which imposes very tangible costs on millions of people in our society.

Politicians—and their advisers—see in Keynes's work an analytic tool shaping economic policy. Keynes's refusal to accept unemployment is a pragmatic call to action. The hydraulic interpretations of Keynes offer the most direct fiscal and monetary policy options. Keynes's pragmatism is also daring. Not everyone makes the step from theoretical speculation to applied policy. Keynes took that step. His daring and commitment are in themselves examples to follow, especially compared to today's passive attitudes.

We see Keynes's pragmatism in 1933. While writing the *General Theory,* he decided not to turn it into a radical reformulation of political economy. He opted instead to frame his insights as an extension of economic theory to the analysis and, as importantly, the solutions for long-term unemployment. This was not a simple, reactive response to the unemployment crisis in Great Britain. Rather, it reflected Keynes's assessment of his own science's role. He had developed a philosophy of economics that made a clean break with established views that tended to see unemployment as on a par with a natural calamity, an inevitability that would right itself in time. Keynes offered a more hopeful view: economic activity is a variable that human beings can control, a variable that depends to a large degree on what agents, as a group, believe they can accomplish, so long as they act together. Subjective beliefs become the principal determinants of objective economic performance. Keynes's *General Theory* was, then, a tool for coordinating beliefs in the interest of making beneficial policies. It was intended to be a rallying point for those who sought to combat unemployment and spur economic growth.

Academic and pragmatic Keynesian approaches to macroeconomics both require creativity and commitment. In our own era of uncertainty, which includes unemployment, resource scarcity, and environmental challenges of daunting scope, these are requisite virtues. Keynes's insights offer solutions to the crises of our own time, if we choose to use them.

Bibliography

Keynes in the Text

Keynes, John. M. *The Collected Writings of J.M. Keynes.* 29 vols. London: Macmillan, St. Martin's Press for the Royal Economic Society, 1971–1983.

Especially:

Vol. 2: *The Economic Consequences of the Peace,* 1919.
Vol. 4: *A Tract on Monetary Reform,* 1923.
Vol. 5: *A Treatise on Money: 1 The Pure Theory of Money,* 1930.
Vol. 6: *A Treatise on Money: 2 The Applied Theory of Money,* 1930.
Vol. 7: *The General Theory of Employment, Interest, and Money,* 1936.
Vol. 8: *A Treatise on Probability,* 1921.
Vol. 10: *Essays in Biography,* 1933.
Vol. 14: *The General Theory and After: Part 2. Defense and Development,* 1973.
———. *General Theory of Employment, Interest, and Money.* New York: Harcourt, 1964: 1936.
———. "The 'Ex-Ante' Theory of the Rate of Interest." *Economic Journal* 47, no. 188 (December 1937): 663–669.
———. "Alternative Theories of the Rate of Interest." *Economic Journal* 47, no. 186 (June 1937): 241–252.
———. "The General Theory of Employment." *Quarterly Journal of Economics* 51, no. 2 (February 1937): 209–223.

Books and Articles

Akerlof, George A. *Efficiency Wage Models of the Labor Market.* New York: Cambridge University Press, 1986.
Arena, R., and D. Torre, eds. *Keynes et les nouveaux keynesiens.* Paris: Presses Universitaires de France, 1993.

Arrous, J. "Keynes et les probabilités, un aspect du fondamentalisme keynesien." *Revue Economique* 33, no. 5 (September 1982): 839–861.

Arrow, Kenneth, and Gerard Debreu, "Existence of an Equilibrium for a Competitive Economy." *Econometrica* 22 (1954): 265–290.

Arrow, Kenneth, Leonid Hurwicz, and H. Block. "On the Stability of the Competitive Equilibrium." *Econometrica* 27 (1959): 82–109.

Azariadis, Costas. "Implicit Contracts and Underemployment Equilibria." *Journal of Political Economy* 83, no. 6 (December 1975): 1183–1202.

Azariadis, Costas, and Roger Guesnerie. "Sunspots and Cycles." *Review of Economic Studies* 53 (1986): 725–737.

Barrère, Alain. "Introduction: Le projet keynesien." In *Keynes aujourd'hui: Théories et politiques,* ed. Alain Barrère and Antoin d'Autume. Paris: Economica, 1985.

Barro, Robert J. "Are Government Bonds Net Wealth?" *Journal of Political Economy* 82, no. 6 (November/December 1974): 1095–1117.

Benassy, Jean-Pascal. "Micro-Economic Foundations and Properties of a Macro-Economic Model." In *Macro-Economics and Imperfect Competition*, ed. Jean-Pascal Benassy. Elgar Reference Collection, International Library of Critical Writings in Economics, 46: 193–210. Aldershot, UK: Elgar, 1995.

———. "Nonclearing Markets: Microeconomic Concepts and Macroeconomic Applications." *Journal of Economic Literature* 31, no. 2 (June 1993): 732–761.

———. *Macroéconomie et théorie de déséquilibre.* Paris: Dunod, 1984.

———. "Théorie du déséquilibre et fondements microéconomiques de la macroéconomie." *Revue Economique* 27, no. 5 (October 1976): 755–804.

———. "Neo-Keynesian Disequilibrium Theory in a Monetary Economy." *Review of Economic Studies* 42, no. 4 (October 1975): 503–523.

Blanchard, Olivier J., and Nobuhiro Kiyotaki. "Monopolistic Competition and the Effect of Aggregate Demand." *American Economic Review* 77 (September 1987): 647–666.

Böhm-Bawerk, Eugen von. *Capital and Interest,* 3 vols. Trans. George Huncke and Hans Sennhotz. South Holland, IL: Libertarian Press, 1959. First published 1884–1889.

Cartelier, J. *L'Economie de Keynes.* Brussels: De Boeck, 1995.

Carnap, Rudolf. *Logical Foundations of Probability.* Chicago: University of Chicago Press, 1950.

Chamberlin, Edward. *The Theory of Monopolistic Competition.* Cambridge, MA: Harvard University Press, 1933.

Clower, Robert, ed. *Monetary Theory.* Harmondsworth, UK: Penguin Modern Economic Readings, 1969.

Coddington, Alex. "Keynesian Economics: The Search of Some Principles." *Journal of Economic Literature* 14, no. 4 (December 1976): 1258–1273.

Cooper, R., and A. John. "Coordinating Coordination Failures in Keynesian Models." *Quarterly Journal of Economics* 103 (August 1998): 441–464.

Davidson, Paul. *Post Keynesian Macroeconomic Theory.* Brookfield, VT: Elgar, 1994.

de Finetti, Bruno. "La prévision, ses lois logiques, ses sources subjectives." *Annales de l'Institut Henri Poincaré* 7 (1937):1–68. English translation in *Studies in Subjective Probability,* ed. Henry E. Kyburg Jr. and Howard E. Smokler. New York: Wiley, 1964.

De Vroey, M. "Involuntary Unemployment: The Missing Piece in Keynes' General Theory." *European Journal of the History of Economic Thought* 4, no. 2 (1997): 284–298.

Domar, Evsey. "Capital Expansion, Rate of Growth, and Employment." *Econometrica* 14, no. 2 (April 1946): 137–147.

Dupuy, Jean-Pierre. *Introduction aux sciences sociales, logique des phénomènes.* Paris: Collectif, Ellipse, 1992.

Eymard-Duvernay, François, and Christian Bessy. *Les intermédiaires du marché du travail.* Paris: Presses Universitaires de France, 1997.

Farmer, Roger E. *The Macroeconomics of Self-Fulfilling Prophecies.* Cambridge, MA: MIT Press, 1993.

Favereau, O. "L'Incertain dans la révolution keynesienne: L'hypothèse Wittengenstein." *Economies et Sociétés* 19, no. 3 (March 1985): 29–72.

Fisher, Irving. *The Theory of Interest as Determined by Impatience to Spend Income and Opportunity to Invest It.* London: Macmillan, 1930.

———. *The Purchasing Power of Money.* London: Macmillan, 1911.

———. *The Rate of Interest: Its Nature, Determination, and Relation to Economic Phenomena.* New York: Macmillan, 1907.

Georgeschu-Roegen, Nicholas. "The Nature of Expectation and Uncertainty," in *Expectations, Uncertainty, and Business Behavior,* ed. Mary Jean Bowman, pp. 11–29. New York: Social Science Research Council, 1958.

Gordon, Robert J. "What Is New-Keynesian Economics?" *Journal of Economic Literature* 28, no. 3 (September 1990): 1115–1171.

Grandmont, J.M. *Monnaie et valeur.* ENSAE Series. Paris: Economica, 1986.

Graziani, A. "The Debate on Keynes' Financing Motive." *Economic Notes* no. 1 (1984): 5–34.

Guesnerie, Roger, and Michael Woodford. "Endogenous Fluctuations." In *Advances in Economic Theory,* ed. J.J. Laffont, 2, pp. 289–412. New York: Cambridge University Press, 1992.

Hansen, Alvin H. *A Guide to Keynes.* New York: McGraw-Hill, 1953.

———. *Monetary Theory and Fiscal Policy.* New York: McGraw-Hill, 1949.

Harrod, Roy F. *Towards a Dynamic Economics: Some Recent Developments of Economic Theory and Their Application to Policy.* London: Macmillan, 1948.

———. "Essay in Dynamic Theory." *Economic Journal* 49 (June 1939): 14–33.

Hayek, Friedrich A. von. *Prices and Production.* Studies in Economics and Political Science, no. 107. London: Routledge, 1931.

Hicks, John R. *Causality in Economics.* New York: Basic Books, 1979.

———. "Mr. Keynes and the Classics: A Suggested Interpretation." *Econometrica* 5, no. 2 (April 1937): 147–159.

Kahn, Richard. "The Financing of Public Works: A Note." *Economic Journal* 42, no. 167 (September 1932): 492–495.

———. "The Relation of Home Investment to Unemployment." *Economic Journal* 41, no. 162 (June 1931): 173–198.

Kaldor, Nicholas. "Capital Accumulation and Economic Growth." In *The Theory of Capital: Proceedings of a Conference Held by the International Economic Association,* ed. F.A. Lutz and D.C. Hague. New York: St. Martin's Press, 1961.

———. "Alternative Theories of Distribution." *Review of Economic Studies* 23, no. 2 (1956): 83–100.

———. "The Relation of Economic Growth and Cyclical Fluctuations." *Economic Journal* 64, no. 253 (March 1954): 53–71.

―――. "Professor Hayek and the Concertina Effect." *Economica* 9 (November 1942): 359–382.

Kaldor, Nicholas, and James Mirrlees. "A New Model of Economic Growth." *Review of Economic Studies* 29, no. 3 (June 1962): 174–192.

Knight, Frank. *Risk, Uncertainty and Profit.* Chicago: University of Chicago Press, 1921.

Kregel, Jan A. "The Microfoundations of the 'Generalization of the General Theory' and 'Bastard Keynesianism': Keynes' Theory in the Long and the Short Period," *Cambridge Journal of Economics* 7, no. 3–4 (September–December 1983): 343–361.

Laplace, Pierre-Simon, Marquis de. *A Philosophical Essay on Probabilities.* Trans. F.W. Truscott and F.L. Emory. New York: J. Wiley, 1902. First published 1814.

Lavoie, Marc. "The Credit-Led Supply of Deposits and the Demand for Money: Kaldor's Reflux Mechanism as Previously Endorsed by Joan Robinson." *Cambridge Journal of Economics* 23, no. 1 (January 1999): 103–113.

―――. "Loanable Funds, Endogenous Money and Minsky's Financial Fragility Hypothesis." In *Money, Financial Institutions and Macroeconomics,* ed. Avi J. Cohen, Harold Hagemann, and John Smithin, pp. 67–82. Boston: Kluwer Academic Press, 1997.

―――. *Foundations of Post-Keynesian Economic Analysis.* Brookfield, VT: Elgar, 1992.

―――."Monnaie et production: Une synthèse de la théorie du circuit." *Economies et Société* 21, no. 9 (September 1987): 65–101.

Leijonhuvfud, A. *On Keynesian Economics and the Economics of Keynes.* New York: Oxford University Press, 1968.

Lucas, Robert. "Economic Policy Evaluation: A Critique." In *The Phillips Curve and Labor Markets,* ed. Karl Brunner and Allan Meltzer, vol. 1, pp.19–46. New York: American Elsevier, 1976.

Malinvaud, E. *Réexamen de la théorie du chômage.* Paris: Calmann-Levy, 1980.

―――. *The Theory of Unemployment Reconsidered.* Oxford: Blackwell, 1977.

Mankiw, Gregory N., and David Romer, eds. *New Keynesian Economics.* 2 vols. Cambridge, MA: MIT Press, 1991.

Marshall, Alfred. *Money, Credit and Commerce.* London: Macmillan, 1923.

―――. *Principles of Economics.* London: Macmillan, 1890.

Menger, Carl. *Principles of Economics: First, General Part.* Glencoe, IL: Free Press, 1950. First published 1871.

Minsky, Hyman P. *Can "It" Happen Again? Essays on Instability and Finance.* New York: M.E. Sharpe, 1982.

Moore, Basil J. *Horizontalists and Verticalists: The Macroeconomics of Credit Money.* New York: Cambridge University Press, 1988.

Myrdal, Gunnar. *Monetary Equilibrium.* New York: Augustus M. Kelley, 1965. First published 1939.

Orléan, André. *Analyse économique des conventions.* Paris: PUF, 1992.

Parguez, Alain. "Financial Markets, Unemployment and Inflation within a Circuitist Framework." *Economies et Sociétés* 30, no. 2–3 (February–March 1996): 163–192.

―――. "La crise dans le circuit, ou l'intégration de la finance et de la production." *Economie Appliquée* 40, no. 4 (1987): 755–770.

Pasinetti, Luigi. *Growth and Income Distribution: Essays in Economic Theory.* Cambridge: Cambridge University Press, 1974.

―――. "Rate of Profit and Income Distribution in Relation to the Rate of Economic Growth," *Review of Economic Studies* 29, no. 4 (October 1962): 267–279.

Patinkin, Don. *Keynes' Monetary Thought: A Study of Its Development.* Durham, NC: Duke University Press, 1976.

————. *Money, Interest and Prices: An Integration of Monetary and Value Theory.* New York: Harper and Row, 1956.

Pigou, Arthur. *Keynes's General Theory: A Retrospective View.* London: Macmillan, 1950.

————. *The Theory of Unemployment.* London: Macmillan, 1933.

————. *Industrial Fluctuations.* London: Macmillan, 1927.

Poulon, F., ed. "Keynes et Robertson: Naissance d'un désaccord." *Economies et Sociétés* 21, no. 9 (September 1987): 9–22.

————. *Les écrits de Keynes.* Paris: Dunod, 1985.

Ramsey, Frank P. "Truth and Probability." In *The Foundations of Mathematics and Other Logical Essays*, ed. R.B. Braitwaite. London: Routledge, 1969. First published 1926.

Robertson, Dennis H. "More Notes on the Rate of Interest." *Review of Economic Studies* 21, no. 2 (1953–1954): 136–141.

————. *Banking Policy and the Price Level.* New York: Augustus M. Kelley, 1949. First published 1926.

————. *Money.* Cambridge: Cambridge University Press, 1948.

Robinson, E.A.G. *The Structure of Competitive Industry.* London: Nisbet, 1931.

Robinson, Joan. *Essays in the Theory of Economic Growth.* London: Macmillan, 1962a.

————. Review of *Money Trade and Economic Growth*, by H.G. Johnson. *Economic Journal* 72, no. 287 (September 1962b): 690–692.

————. *The Accumulation of Capital.* Homewood, IL: Irwin, 1956.

————. *The Economics of Imperfect Competition.* London: Macmillan, 1969. First published 1933.

Salais, Robert. *L'invention du chômage: Histoire et transformations d'une catégorie en France des années 1890 aux années 1980.* Paris: Presses Universitaires de France, 1999.

Salais, Robert, and Noel Whiteside, eds. *Governance, Industry, and Labour Markets in Britain and France: The Modernising State in the Mid-twentieth Century.* New York: Routledge, 1998.

Samuelson, Paul A. *Economics.* New York: McGraw-Hill, 1973.

Savage, Leonard. *The Foundations of Statistics.* Mineola, NY: Dover Publications, 1954.

Say, Jean-Baptiste. *A Treatise on Political Economy.* Trans. C.R. Prinsep. New York: A.M. Kelly, 1964. First published 1803.

Schmitt, Bernard. "A New Paradigm for the Determination of Money Prices." In *Money in Motion: The Post-Keynesian and Circulation Approaches*, ed. Ghislain Deleplace and Edward J. Nell, pp. 104–138. Jerome Levy Economics Institute Series. New York: St. Martin's Press, 1996. London: Macmillan, 1996.

————. "The Identity of Aggregate Supply and Demand in Time." In *The Foundations of Keynesian Analysis: Proceedings of a Conference Held at the University of Paris I–Pantheon-Sorbonne*, ed. Alain Barrère, pp. 169–193. New York: St. Martin's Press, 1988.

Shackle, George L. *Time, Expectations, and Uncertainty in Economics: Selected Essays of G.L.S. Shackle.* Brookfield, VT: Elgar, 1990.

————. *The Years of High Theory.* New York: Cambridge University Press, 1967.

————. *Uncertainty in Economics, and Other Reflections.* Cambridge: Cambridge University Press, 1955.

Skidelsky, Robert. *John Maynard Keynes.* London: Macmillan, 1992.

Sonnenschein, Hugo. "Do Walras' Identity and Continuity Characterize the Class of Community Excess Demand?" *Journal of Economic Theory* 6, no. 4 (August 1973): 345–354.

Sraffa, Piero. *Production of Commodities by Means of Commodities: Prelude to a Critique of Economic Theory.* Cambridge: Cambridge University Press, 1960.

———. "The Laws of Return under Competitive Conditions." *Economic Journal* 36 (1926): 535–550. French translation in Sraffa, Piero, *Ecrits d'économie politique.* Paris: Economica, 1926.

Stiglitz, Joseph E. "Price Rigidities and Market Structure." *American Economic Review* 74 (May 1984): 350–355.

Stiglitz, Joseph E., and Bruce Greenwald. "New and Old Keynesians." In *A Macroeconomics Reader,* ed. Brian Snowdon and Howard R. Vane, pp. 552–574. New York: Routledge, 1997.

Stiglitz, Joseph E., and Andrew Weiss. "Credit Rationing in Markets with Imperfect Information." *American Economic Review* 71 (June 1981): 393–410.

Thévenot, Laurent. "A propos de la notion de convention," in *L'Economie des conventions: débat critique,* ed. Philippe Bernoux. Lyon: Groupe Lyonnais de Sociologie Industrielle and Maison Rhône-Alpes des Sciences de l'Homme, 1993.

Thévenot, L., and P. Livet. "Les catégories de l'action collective." In *Analyse économique des conventions,* ed. A. Orléan. Paris: Presses Universitaires de France, 1994.

Tobin, James. "Notes on Optimal Monetary Growth." *Journal of Political Economy* 76, no. 4, (July–August 1968): 833–859.

———. "Commercial Banks as Creators of Money." In *Banking and Monetary Studies,* ed. D. Carson. Homewood, IL: Irwin, 1963.

———. "Liquidity Preference as Behavior Towards Risk." *Review of Economic Studies* 25, no. 2. (February 1958): 65–86.

———. "The Interest-Elasticity of Transactions Demand for Cash." *Review of Economics and Statistics* 38, no. 3 (August 1956): 241–247.

Turgeon, Lynn. "L'incertitude Keynesienne et le projet pragmatique: L'hypothèse de l'instrumentalisme scientifique." *Economie et société* 31, no. 10 (October 1997): 115–134.

———. *Bastard Keynesianism: The Evolution of Economic Thinking and Policymaking Since World War II.* Westport, CT: Greenwood, 1996.

Ventelou, Bruno. "La réalité existe-t-elle: Keynes premier économiste constructiviste," *Réseau-Revue de Philosophie Morale et Politique*, 2002 octobre.

———. *Au delà, la croissance économique comme construction sociale.* Paris: Albin Michel, 2001.

Vercelli, Allessandro. *Methodological Foundations of Macroeconomics: Keynes and Lucas.* Cambridge: Cambridge University Press, 1991.

Wald, Abraham. "On Some Systems of Equations of Mathematical Economics," trans. Otto Eckstein, *Econometrica* 19 (1951): 368–403.

———. "Über einige Gleichungssysteme der mathematischen Ökonomie," *Zeitschrift für Nationalökonomie* 6, no. 5 (1936): 637–670.

Walras, Léon. *Elements of Pure Economics: Or, the Theory of Social Wealth.* American Economic Association Translation Series. London: Allen and Unwin, 1954. First published 1874.

Weintraub, Sidney. "The Keynesian Theory of Inflation: The Two Faces of Janus." *International Economic Review* 1, no. 2 (1960): 143–155.

Wicksell, Knut. *Lectures on Political Economy.* London: Routledge, 1906.

Index

About the Author and Translator

Bruno Ventelou studied as an undergraduate at the Ecole Normale Supérieure de Cachan, where he later taught, and completed his doctoral work at the Ecole des Hautes Etudes en Sciences Sociales. He held a position at the Institut d'Etudes Politiques in Paris. His published work includes the present volume, which was first published in France by Vuibert in 1997 as *Lire Keynes et le Comprendre*. His second book, *Au-delà de la Rareté* (*Beyond Scarcity*) was published in 2001. His professional publications cover three areas: the economics of corruption and its significance for growth and development theories; Keynesian economic theory and macroeconomic policies; and the economics of health policy. He currently works for the Institut National de la Santé et de la Recherche Médicale, where he directs a research team on public health systems and economic regulation.

Gregory P. Nowell teaches international political economy at the State University of New York at Albany. His research interests and publications have touched upon the Smithian, Marxian, and Weberian theories of capitalist development; the work of the English theorist and polemicist John Hobson; and the international oil market. He is the author of *Mercantile States and the World Oil Cartel, 1900–1939* (1994). He has published articles in *Barron's,* the Dow Jones financial weekly, and also the *Journal of Post-Keynesian Economics*.